BOOK ONE

THE ITALIAN INFLUENCE
ON
WESTERN LAW AND CULTURE

BOOK TWO

THE ITALIAN INFLUENCE
ON THE
SPREAD OF CHRISTIANITY

PHILIP A. RAPISARDA

DEDICATED TO THE
MEMORY OF
BLANCHE C. RAPISARDA

A special salute to the Associated Italian-American Charities, Inc.
A volunteer group of conscientious and dedicated men doing God's work in
a business-like manner.

Copyright 1992 Philip A. Rapisarda, Baltimore, Maryland
All rights reserved Philip A. Rapisarda - Publisher, Baltimore Maryland
No part may be copied or reproduced without permission of the author.
First Revision 1993
Library of Congress Catalog Card No. 93-092822
ISBN 0-9642512-0-5

Acknowledgements

Mary E. Oppitz - Typing from original notes
Janet L. Seward - Proofreading and arrangement
Stacey A. Seward - Artwork and calligraphy
Charlotte Hatcher - Typing and semi final draft
Patricia W. Boyd - Word processing final draft

Table of Contents

Preface
Dedication to Blanche C. Rapisarda

PREFACE

This treatise did not begin with a title followed by a text. Actually, the title came last.

After graduation from law school and recalling my pre-law history studies, my curiosity was sparked by the remarkable similarity between the ancient Roman Republic form of government and that of our own. The three branches of government, their powers and limitations, were too much alike to be coincidental.

Further study of this improbability took the turn of study into their laws. This was a real eye-opener. Reviewing ancient Roman Law was a "back to the future" experience of Twentieth Century law. Likewise, there was an uncanny similarity between ancient Roman Law and many of our laws and legal principles in effect today.

It immediately raised the question: Are we that far behind, or were they that far ahead of their time? The difference in time is over 2,000 years! My interest further aroused, I searched for additional topics typical of this oddity. Others were uncovered and furthermore, there appeared to be a decided flow of forces at work that influenced the development of Western Culture. Drawn further into this "discovery," I decided to record my notes under the title of The Influence of Italians on Western Culture. much as you might find similar works of Egyptian, Babylonian, or Greek influences on Western Culture.

To test if this was a "dry hole" subject, I initiated conversation with students at a college library and inquired if they had ever heard of Enrico Fermi or Cicero. Only one student thought Fermi was "some kind of scientist" while the others either never heard of him or thought he was the author of The Godfather. All of them had heard of Cicero, as an ancient Roman, but none of them knew of any particular distinction concerning him.

I decided to gather more information on all of the topics, but personal matters interrupted my studies until recently.

The topics selected are normally extensive subjects in themselves. Therefore, the discourses herein are limited to the title and are brief. It is hoped, however, that there is sufficient data for others with similar interests to seek further study.

PHILIP A. RAPISARDA, 1992

INTRODUCTION

It may appear out of the ordinary to have a treatise with this title and then introduce it with a praise of Greece, but that is what we must do.

Much of where world civilization is today can be traced to the legacy of Greek thinkers, artists, and the creativity of its people.

This treatise attempts to emphasize the Roman/Italian <u>Influence</u> on Western Culture (not its originator).

Scholarly studies rarely attempt to seek out the very first uttering of an original concept or idea. Usually it disappears into anonymity, or into the mist of time. For example, the old saying "Spare the rod and spoil the child" is etched into the wall of an Egyptian temple in hieroglyphics, but who was its author? Rome, exposed to the philosophies and the art of Greece, combined it with their own and with their practicality for implementation, put them in the forefront of world leadership.

Cicero agrees and, referring to the Greeks, says ". . . from whom we owe so much." Cicero also admits that his philosophies are not original, but followed Greek thinking.

Actually, there was very little really new in early written form of Italian philosophy. Italian philosophy was expressed more in a visual sense through themes of art and religion than in written form.

In the Roman pursuit of their ideals, they appear to have only their own agenda in mind. They hold to their own ideas, which they thought were best, to the exclusion of all others. This seems especially so in the matter of the Roman XII Tables of Laws. The Decemviri, 10 Roman lawyers who toured the known world to study their laws, compounded a set of laws based almost totally on their own custom, usage, and traditions. Any principle of law acquired elsewhere was lost or merged into their own. Consequently, scholars investigating this subject conclude that the XII Tables are unquestionably of Roman origin.

The early and high development of Greek Culture and Philosophy gives credence to their influence on Roman Culture. Notwithstanding this, the preponderance, longevity, and quality of Roman Culture took on a life of its own causing a fading of prior history in comparison.

Author Leonard Cottrell writes, "Rome was unlike any other state then existing in the world . . . long ago it had been ruled by kings, but got rid of them and was now a Republic---its Rulers, the Senate, were elected." (113 p. 22)

The Italian legacy and influence on Western Culture is well documented scholastically, but it is scattered. This treatise attempts to combine what is considered the most important topics put under one cover. Some readers will no doubt feel that there are other influences that could have been included, but any subject covering a span of over 2,500 years would obviously have many more possible topics. The limitation herein is to focus on Italian influences.

It is interesting to note that at almost every pivotal juncture in the development of Western Culture, Italians played a significant part. The topics included here are of a more secular nature, although some aspects concerning justice, fairness, and the goodness of mankind, in a sense, come close to spirituality.

The subject of Religion, Book II (Christianity in particular) will be made a study at another time and combined herewith. Italians, with their vitality and strong faith, were a significant factor in the spread of Christianity throughout the world.

NOTE: The American Republic is a child of the Roman Republic. The United States Constitution has been hailed as the greatest document ever created for the purpose of establishing a workable government of the people, for the people, under the format of a Republic, and including a protective system of Checks and Balances.

At the time the Founding Fathers were at work on this plan, the mother country, England, was ruled by a king who believed he received his right by divine intervention. It's absolutism was painfully oppressive, and took two wars to break the bonds.

The delegates to the United States Constitutional Convention had to look elsewhere for a model starting point. To this end, "They were wise enough to tap the experience of the ancients." (Grollier's Encyclopedia, 1970 Edition, p. 146-U) They relied heavily on the Roman System.

With this brief preamble, the example of the ancient Roman Republic begins its rise from the mist of time to play a modern part. (Refer to Appendix herein for comparisons) Its influence on our system is further detailed in the following text.

A detailed bibliography is included to encourage further study.

Philip A. Rapisarda

BOOK 1

The
Italian Influence on
Western Law and Culture

Important:

It is important to remember when recalling the Roman Empire, that there were two periods of the Empire totaling about one thousand years. The first period was the early Roman Republic (about 500 B.C. to 50 B.C.) and was a government of the people, more or less, with Consuls, Senators and Tribunes. (Tribunes were the representatives of the people and elected by the people. Refer to the Appendix herein.)

When the American Forefathers met to devise a system of government with the all important feature of "checks and balances," it was the early Roman Republic system of government that was used as a model.

The later period of the Roman Empire was the period when the government was taken over and controlled by the military and emperors. (they are often erroneously lumped together and referred to as "Caesars.") This period also lasted about five hundred years to about 550 A.D.

Even though the Roman Empire was controlled by emperors, many of the old civil rights laws of the Republic were retained. One of the more important ones being the right of Habeas Corpus. (The right of an accused to be brought to and have an audience before the emperor.)

Herein, when we refer to the laws and the system of government of Rome, we are of course referring to those of the early Roman Republic.

PART I. THE EARLY INFLUENCE

Italians have played a major part in the rise and spread of our Western Culture, first in the rise of Roman Civilization and again in the Italian Renaissance. As for civilization and culture, what is it? It has been said, "whatever it is, I know it when I see it." The enormous volume of scholastic material on Roman Civilization, law, and culture clearly documents in a thousand ways its legacy to later generations. It is in the genes of Western Culture and we, the beneficiaries, are much the better for it.

In the development and progress of nationalization, Italy was the first European country to become an organized state." ...Rome, the first nation to conceive and then carry out a process of political unification that subordinated local to national loyalties."(1) The 19th century historian, Leopold Von Ranke wrote, "All modern history stems from Rome and had Rome not existed, there would be no history to speak of." (2) Petrarch, the 12th Century poet and philosopher, said "What is history, other than the praise of Rome." This exaggeration has a certain element of truth to it. Roman characteristics, deep in resources of vitality, intelligence, imagination, and human compassion, have placed them on the cutting edge of the development of Western Culture, and it has spread to virtually every other culture in the world. This spread continues today with renewed vigor and strength. Future generations in less developed parts of the world may some day trace their concepts of law and government back to the above sources.

These ideals flowing abundantly from Rome were no mere accident of human nature. The ideals and philosophies in their obscure ancient history existed long before the advent of Rome. The same may be said of their other talents in art and architecture. However, they took root in the fertile minds and the vitality of the Romans who gave them meaning and provided the momentum to effect their spread.

No ideal (save Christianity) has captured the mind of mankind as did the Roman principles of law and government. To appreciate the magnitude of this, one has only to view events of the current generation. Communism, brainchild of Marx, Engles and Lenin, was touted to be the "Wave of the Future." It crashed and rippled on the beach in only 70 years. Hitler's Reich, "built to last a thousand years," lasted only ten. Virtually every concept of government has faded from the scene save those given by the legacy of Rome. After 2000 years they still carry on with strength and effectiveness in modified form. (see Appendix)

However, the Empire was not without its faults. The history of the decline of the Empire has been documented, and its causes theorized in a thousand books. The Empire was of such singular importance in the world and its decline so traumatic to the world, that Gibbon wrote. "The fall of Rome was the greatest, and perhaps most awful scene in the history of mankind."(3) Will Durant says similarly, "The rise and fall of Rome is surely the greatest drama ever played by man."(3a) However, this writing is not intended to indulge in the history of the Empire, but to focus on the forces and certain ideals of its laws and system of government that were put in motion by it. Its principles of government, law and justice were so firmly established in the heart and memory of mankind that after Rome's fall, (through Italy's gift of the Renaissance 1000 years later) the idealism of its past rose again. In any study of this topic, it is Roman legal principles and its system of government that are most universally agreed upon by scholars as the "legacy of Rome" to Western Culture. "Justice, the desire and thirst of all mankind, perhaps the single most unquenchable desire, was a Roman invention codified in the Roman XII tables of law." (4) (5) (6) (Refer to the details of the XII tables of law under that heading.)

The Early Formation of the Republic:

The early Greeks, by their creation of the principles of democracy, prepared the groundwork for those who sought rule by the will of the people and not by the absolutism of a monarchy. This was followed by the founding of the Roman Republic in about 500 B.C. Under King Servius Tullius, two Consuls were engaged to assist him and were elected annually. Each Consul had equal power with authority to counter the acts of the other, which was an elementary form of "checks and balances." (7) When a Senate was later founded, its makeup was so intellectually impressive that the ambassador from Pyrrhus described it as an "assembly of Kings." (8) The system of government was further developed to a bicameral legislative form by adding an Assembly of The People whose representatives were called Tribunes. Tribunes had the power to stop any action of the Senate by crying out "Veto." (I forbid)

This power furthered the effectiveness of the idea of "checks and balances." The executive power was shared by the two Consuls, and they were assisted and advised by the Senate which was responsible for finance and foreign policy. The Assembly of the

People made the laws and also had veto power over the acts of the Senate. The principle of "checks and balances" in government was often duplicated through the ages, down to the founding of the American system of government, and this protection was incorporated into our Constitution. "We too, whose Constitution was shaped by men who knew their Roman authors well, should consider Rome's enduring influence." (10)

It bears repeating that while this brief account cannot possibly pass for a history of Rome, certain aspects of its characteristics must be described if we are to understand the impact and spread of its civilizing influence, and quotations must be referred to frequently in support of them.

That the populations of the Empire readily accepted the Roman principles of justice was an obvious conclusion and aided immeasurably to its spread. "The Empire of Rome comprehended the fairest part of the earth and the most civilized portion of mankind." (13) Winston Churchill stated similarly, "Where Caesar conquered, civilization dwelt." (14) (15)

As Romanization spread across western Europe, the conquered tribes learned to live as Romans. Land was cultivated, Roman engineers drained marshes, and built sanitation and water supply aqueducts. "Water supply as such was not enjoyed again in Europe before the nineteenth century." (16)

The Romans built broad, straight roads and bridges. Servants of the emperor rode 80 kilometers per day carrying orders to provincial governors all over the Empire. The people elected their own leaders and they became autonomous to a degree. (17)

"The journey of a Roman official from Asia minor to Italy in fourteen days over the splendid roads of the Roman Empire, was not duplicated any where in America or Europe until the year 1800." (18) (Refer to illustration of road system)

Western Europe was completely Roman. The East remained Greek in language and feeling, but Roman law and government prevailed there. (19)

Rome was of such a unique achievement that some historians questioned what it was that made them what they were. Of the many ingredients suggested, the characteristic most often mentioned was the Roman-Italian faith and trust in a principle based on fairness and justice. They resisted change, always believing that their old ways were best. The typical Roman-Italian was a "conservative" and strove to be a "gentleman." In his own eyes, he was the model of an upright, unsentimental maker of things, and a mover of events. (20)

A consensus of readings on these matters depicts the Romans as seeing themselves as what might be called a modern day gentleman. The Greeks were greatly admired and viewed as being artistic, casual, and less inhibited than Romans. (21) Romans recognized and praised the Greeks for their refinement.

"A Roman gentleman strove to create the impression of being a reserved spectator, not for him was the sweaty rolling in the dust of a gymnasium." (22) Concerning the activities of the "Roman Gentleman," Cicero wrote, "Public opinion divides the trades and professions into the liberal and the vulgar." According to Cicero, "The least respectable of all trades are those which minister to pleasure." (23) These characterizations are hardly the customary picture of a Roman citizen who is usually depicted in our media as a whip - swinging oppressor. It would appear that by Cicero's description it more aptly fits the modern image of an "English Gentleman." There has never been any question that there were weaknesses (as in any large cosmopolitan society,) but the depravity depicted today in novels and movies is due to the wide latitude given to authors and script writers. (24) Domestic peace and a sense of union were the natural consequences of Roman policy.

The Monarchies of Asia were for the most part, despotic and harsh in the treatment of their subjects. Obedience was harshly enforced. Not so in the Roman Empire. Obedience was voluntary and the people scarcely considered their own existence as not being a Roman, and a sense of fairness and justice prevailed. The emperor's authority was exercised with the same uniformity and fairness in every province of the Empire. Roman legions were there to protect the population from outsiders and not to mistreat the populace. (25) In most instances, the military was stationed outside the perimeter of the locale.

The population flocked to Rome, eager to come under the protection of its laws. From the makeup of its swelling volume of population, the City of Rome could be considered the world's first "melting pot." Rome was filled with subjects and strangers from every part of the world. "In great part, provincials were granted Roman citizenship. Gifted provincials gained honor throughout the Empire, some of Rome's greatest writers and best emperors were provincials. (26) "Rome's idea of imperialism was to educate and encourage able and ambitious provincials to seek careers with the very highest posts open to them in the Central Imperial Administration." (27) The narrow policy of preserving the pure blood of its citizens hastened the ruin of nearby city-states. "Rome deemed it more prudent to adopt virtue and merit, whether found among slaves or strangers, enemies, or barbarians." (28) The unification of such diverse provinces created problems of such magnitude that later in the empire changes had to be made to adapt. "While they may suffer from an occasional partial abuse of delegated power, the general principles of government were wise, simple and beneficial." (29)

Rome gradually allowed freedom of the city to all worshipers - of any kind. "The interests of the Priests and beliefs of the people were sufficiently respected. They often engaged in the ceremonies of the inhabitants and frequented their temples, subverting their own beliefs to the local laws and customs. Such was the intelligence of their governing." (30) "They knew and valued the advantages of religion as it connected with civil government, and they encouraged public festivals which humanize the manners of the people. Only in the instance of human sacrifice (by the Druids in England) was this policy excepted." (31) However, during the period when some of the early emperors took on the added title of "Emperor and God," Christians were persecuted for refusing to worship and make sacrifices to them as a "God."

The society that was Rome was in place long enough to change the course of human history. Unlike other empires, Rome's 500 year Republic produced the most profound changes in world history. To make such worldwide changes requires not only the benefit of longevity, but more importantly, it requires a culture that is receptive to the dreams and aspirations of mankind.

The heart of this Roman ethic was in essence its development and adherence to the principle of "Natural Law;" a basic element of humanity. This, therefore, was the heart and center of Roman culture; not perfect, but far to the beneficial side.

While Greek advances in government, philosophy and art were impressive and predated that of Rome, they lacked the benefit of conversion and consolidation. Rome had a talent for governing that was new to the world at that time.
(Note on time frame)
The Constitutional Republic of Rome lasted about 500 years. The empire of Rome (caesars and emperors) lasted another 500 years until the empire fell. During this period many of the civil laws of the former Republic were retained thus providing future generations a legacy of 1,000 years of enlightened jurisprudence.

PART II. ROME'S LEGACY TO WESTERN LAW AND CULTURE

"The study of Rome is a prerequisite to any serious understanding of the Development of Western Civilization." (32) "No other city has cast such a spell on men's minds." (33) "Rome has so dominated mens bodies and minds, for so many centuries, that it has become difficult to imagine a world without Rome." (34)

As mentioned previously, the mere origination of an idea is not the end in itself. It takes more. It needs refinement and implementation for it to effect its benefits. It was such with the Italian-Romans and their system of laws. Mankind must have always dreamed of tranquility and justice. There were societies in existence thousands of years before the time of the Italian-Roman era, but it was the Italian-Romans who put this in motion and it gave birth to the modern world.

". . .The Roman mind is still at work, profoundly influencing our politics, our diplomacy, our art, and literature, our religious and philosophic attitudes, and our laws." (35) If there are any striking achievements by mankind in the long history of his cultures, it is the development and cultivation of law.

Law school teaches that a Nation is made up of three elements: The land, the people, and its laws. The first two elements were there, in place, everywhere in the world. The Italian-Romans provided the essential third ingredient. After that, everything else started to happen. They possessed an innate spirit of fairness with the intelligence and the imagination to create and effect it. Their creation was not just rhetoric, but rhetoric with action.

The XII Tables of Law

In about 450 B.C., the Roman Senate chose a committee of ten men [*Decemviri*] to frame and codify just and equitable laws to govern the newly founded Roman Republic. (America's founding fathers at the Constitutional Convention did likewise in 1788-89.) The outcome of this effort was the creation of the XII Tables of Law, the earliest statute or code of Roman Law. (36) (History credits them as being a Roman invention.) They were composed of laws and customs of ancient Roman usage with the addition of the then current needs principally demanded by the people (Plebeians) who felt that most Senatorial judgements favored the upper classes (Patricians.) (37)

For the first time it recognized the equality of all citizens before the law which was a significant reversal of the despotism of the past under ancient kings. Over a long period of time these laws were expanded to provide more protection for the people and to provide a more open legal system. These laws combined with customs, traditions, and other written laws became what was known as the Roman Constitution. In time, Roman law became exact, impartial, liberal, and humane." (38)

Some of the provisions of the XII Tables of Law will help explain their universal acceptance, and make them recognizable in this 20th Century.

Table I - Trials
1.　　If plaintiff summons a defendant to court, he shall go.
2.　　If he does not go - then only shall he take defendant by force.

Table II - Trials
Whoever is in need of evidence, he shall go - to call out loudly before witnesses' doorway. (To summon a witness)

Table III　Law of Debt

When a debt has been acknowledged, or a judgement about the matter pronounced in court, thirty days must be the legitimate time of grace. (much like our present day 30 day right to appeal.)

Table IV - Right of Head of Family
A child born ten months after the death of the father will not be admitted into a legal inheritance.

Table V - Guardianship-Succession
If a person dies intestate, and has no self successor (meaning another head of family) the nearest agnate (older relative) kinsmen shall have possession of deceased's household. Clansmen shall have possession of his household, if he has no agnates.

Table VI - Acquisition and Possession
When a person shall make a contract or conveyance and the terms are of a verbal declaration, they are to be held binding (As today, a verbal contract is binding in some instances.)

Table VII - Rights Concerning Land

> If a water course directed through a public place shall do damage to a private person, he shall have right of suit to the effect that damage shall be repaired by the owner. (Same as today with the public laying of water lines.)

Table VIII - Torts or Delicts
1. If a four footed animal shall be said to have caused a loss, legal action - shall either surrender of the thing which is causing the damage or offer assessment for the damage. (Such as cows damaging a neighbor's crop)
2. A person who has cut down another person's trees, shall pay twenty-five pieces for every tree.
3. Penalty - for false witness - a person who has been found guilty of giving false witness, shall be hurled down from the Tarpein rock.

Table IX - Public Law
Putting to death - of any man - who has not been convicted is forbidden (Later, the death penalty was all but forbidden for a freeman.)

Table X - Sacred Law
1. Him, whose teeth shall have been fastened with gold - if a person shall bury or burn him with gold, it shall be without punishment.
2. No pyre or personal burning-mound must be erected nearer than sixty feet to another person's building without consent of the owner.

Table XI - (Not applicable to today's laws)

Table XII Pledged property may be seized for nonpayment of debt.

The above examples are from: (39)

Their fascination is also due, in part, to the fact that they are essentially the laws we live by today, slightly modified to our current needs. Consider also, that many of the laws of the XII Tables (not only the above mentioned selections) were very old and were carried down from ancient usage and custom of Rome's earlier centuries and combined with these twelve. These laws were compounded against a backdrop of a world ruled by depostic leaders, where man's inhumanity to man was a daily event. The enlightenment of the Romans becomes ever so apparent. It took a great deal of confidence to put it in writing and into practice. It provides a startling comparison with other peoples and their leaders of the known world, not only at that time, but also today. The spread of this legal philosophy explains the ready acceptance of the peoples of the conquered provinces and for their willingness to accept "Romanization." These laws with their later modifications, interpretations, and codifications became the law of Rome for 1000 years, (40) and then spread throughout the world.

The further liberalization of some provisions provided:

a. Justice was defined as "The steady and abiding purpose to give to every man that which is his own." (41) (Also see "Institutes" following herein)

b. Protecting a child against a father's tyranny.

c. Limiting use of torture to induce a confession.

d. A master who killed a slave should be punished as a murderer.

e. That all men were originally free by law of nature and that therefore slavery be contrary to natural right. (There was an exception where enemies were captured in time of war)

f. An early form of Habeas Corpus. (42)
Right of Habeas Corpus: St. Paul (captured by a mob in Jerusalem) was in danger of being lynched, but as a Roman Citizen he demanded the right to be transported to Rome to stand trial before a Roman Magistrate. (Eerdman's Handbook History of Christianity, p.63)

Further Development of Roman Law

Detailed above are examples of early laws set out in the Roman XII Tables and "seed laws" that underwent continued development as a result of cases, opinions of jurists and lawyers, until they encompassed a comprehensive body of Roman Civil Law. In 550 A.D., under Emperor Justinian, a commission (with the assistance of Emperor Justinian himself) arranged in scientific form the body of civil law known as the "Justinian Code." This became the foundation of the legal system of modern Italy, Spain, France, Germany, and other European countries. These principles also influenced the Common Law of England which America has adopted. It is in effect (as basic law) in the Louisiana, Quebec territories formerly under French control and all Spanish-American countries. As basic law, it also extends to "parts of Asia and Africa." (43)

The laws of the XII Tables were the seed from which the Roman Civil Law grew to maturity and further developed into Roman Jurisprudence. Livey (ancient historian) declared that they (XII Tables) were the fountain of all private and public law. Cicero (famous Roman lawyer and consul) also had great praise for the "XII Tables." Scholars have since said that as a basis and source of law it may well compare with the Constitution of the United States. (44) "They mark the beginning of what was to be Rome's greatest gift to civilization, its legal system." (45) "The Code was genuinely Roman in Content." "In theory the Code remained the foundation of Roman law for 1000 years." (46) ". . . the written law of Emperor Justinian (Justinian Code) still forms the basis of Western Law." (47)

The following are some later and more popular Roman Civil Law provisions that were incorporated into 20th Century American Jurisprudence: (In addition to those of the Roman XII Tables of Law)

1. No one is compelled to defend a cause against his will.
2. No one suffers a penalty for what he thinks.
3. No one may be forcibly removed from his own home.
4. Anything not permitted the defendant ought not to be allowed the plaintiff.
5. The burden of proof is upon the party affirming, not upon the party defending. (Our presumption of innocence doctrine)
6. The gravity of a past offense never increases "ex-post-facto."
7. In inflicting penalties, the age and innocence of the guilty party must be taken into account.
8. In a rule of a "sale" unless there is express agreement to the contrary, the risk of accidental destruction or damage to the object passes to the buyer as soon as the contract was made. (48)
9. If a house were destroyed by an earthquake, the buyer nevertheless had to pay for it. (48)
10. The occupant of a house must not be disturbed and should live in peace. (48)
*11. The accused had the right to confront his accusers. pp. 194-195
*12. Anonymous accusers were not permitted. pp. 194-195

*13.   False accusers were to be punished. p. 66

*14.   Defendant was innocent until proven guilty. p. 66

*15.   Roman citizens were given the right to practice their own religion beginning in 313 A.D. p. 142

*11-15 are found in *Christians And The Roman Empire* by Marta Sordi of Milan, Italy. Translated by Anabel Beldini, University of Oklahoma Press, Norman Oklahoma 1986.

France's Napoleonic Code, German Law, (when not in conflict with local law,) and English Common Law (which was based on precedent rather than written law) all had their roots in the Roman principles of law.

In modified form, the above are still fundamental laws of the Twentieth Century in America.

Professor Raffaelle Dizenzo, (Loyola University Chicago) writing in the *Italian Journal* [1991-#526 Vol. V page 49] points out, ". . .Emperor Justinian, with his Codexiuris, is depicted on the doors of the United States Supreme Court Building in Washington D.C., and the Writ of "Habeas Corpus" the cornerstone of our Civil Liberties is a legal procedure handed down by Roman Law." (49)

Scholars have described Roman Law as being the most admirable system of Jurisprudence ever framed by man.

The logic of their jurisprudence discloses an amazing appreciation and enlightened understanding of legal fundamentals applicable to private, family, and business matters.

Cicero
The Father of His Country
His Law, Oratory, Government

When we think of Rome, Julius Caesar always comes to mind. This is fair enough since he was a great leader and one of the greatest military men the world has ever known. However, side by side, Cicero in many respects, stands taller. This is especially so when making inquiry into Italian Influence on Western Culture . This phase of history cannot be reviewed without reference to Marcus Tullius Cicero.

Marcus Tullius Cicero of Apirnum, Italy (forty miles north of Rome,) 106-43 B.C. is a substantial subject in itself, and his library references are extensive. Biographers praise him as "the supreme index to his age, and that he is in contact with all its interests. His works form a history of his lex, its politics, and society, as well as its literature and knowledge." (50) "There lived the most distinguished letter-writer the world has everknown, one of Rome's very great men, Cicero, the orator."(51) He provided the basic principles for future statesmen to follow in establishing good governments based on law. He was a remarkable man and a legend in his own time. Too often the greatness and ability of a man and his efforts are recognized only after he passes on. This was not so with Cicero. He was a giant among lawyers and was feared as well for his oratorical skill. He was foremost in his ability to persuade and sway an audience, and his oratorical ability was such that any opposing party was, at the outset, considered the underdog. He was also a serious practitioner of the idea that political power in a Constitutional Republic must be achieved through persuasion rather than violence. This principle has been the ideal goal of every Republic ever since and his theories, with reference to law and Republican Form of government, heavily influenced the laws of England and America. He was the prime exponent of Natural Law. (note: in the recent U.S. Senate hearings on Supreme Court nominee Judge Clarence Thomas, when pressed on his legal views, always took the position of his belief in Natural Law, which of course is unassailable. In doing so, he was safe from criticism on that point.)

The following is a translation of Cicero's discourse on Natural Law: "There is in fact a true law, namely, right reason, which is in accordance with nature, applies to all men and is unchangeable and eternal. By its commands, this law summons men to the performance of their duties; by its prohibitions it restrains them from doing wrong. This law arises from the very nature of mankind itself, meaning respect for life and property, good faith and fair dealing." (52)

Black's Law Dictionary rephrases Natural Law as: "Used in the philosophical speculations of Roman Jurists and was intended to denote a system of rules and principles for the guidance of human conduct which might be discovered by <u>rational intelligence of man, would conform and grow out of his nature his whole mental, moral, and physical constitution</u>." (53)

Professor Charles R. Kesler (Claremont College, California) in his speech (at Col. U. in New York) concisely to the point declares: "Cicero was the first Natural Law theorist in the Western tradition. Rejecting Plato's "Utopianism" and Aristotle's doctrines on "Natural Right", Cicero is the first to call political philosophy to the direct and public aid of good government. He does this by articulating a standard of natural law by which good men and decent governments should be guided. He thus launches the tradition of gentlemen-statesmen founding governing Republics under the aegis of a Natural Law teaching." According to professor Kesler, <u>"the political philosophy of Cicero remained largely in books until the American Founding Fathers, who were philosophically literate statesmen, erected new governments in the name of Natural Law"</u>. (54) In the Roman Senate, Cicero was a staunch defender of the constitution and Republican form of government. His position was on the side of Natural Law and government by rhetorical persuasion and against him were the "power bosses." This put him in an endless struggle which ultimately cost him his life.

He was one of the most famous lawyers known to the world, ancient or modern, and his oratory is a model for the successful modern lawyer. The Founding Fathers of America were quick to admit his influence upon their own development of oratory and the principles of law that Cicero expounded. In Cicero's constant defense of the Republic under the Law (and not of dictators), he earned the title of the Father of his Country.

Cicero possessed a brilliant legal mind coupled with a gifted oratorical talent and he derived his greatest satisfaction in guiding the Senate to his way of thinking by his persuasiveness. He was the first Roman to codify the laws (in 18 volumes in 50 B.C.) arranged according to subject. (Note: Today, our own laws follow the same format, codification according to subjects.)

Cicero was also called The Father of Roman Law (55) and has been referred to as a truly modern lawyer/statesman, trapped in the skin of an ancient. He was ahead of his time. The connection between Roman culture, Rome's laws and Cicero's influence begins to emerge. The great body of knowledge is there in libraries, but is rarely brought into the light for purpose of examining its principles; unless one is particularly researching the subject.

Before we take up the formation of the American system of government, it would be helpful to examine the talent and characteristic of Cicero which helps explain his influence on the outcome. Fate placed him, at that time, in the midst of a Roman Republican form of government which was a new concept in governmental form. He had personally developed his talent for oratory and was using it to persuade others to follow or perform, rather than to use force. He perfected it to a high degree and practiced it daily as he developed his style. His philosophical beliefs, from a practical sense, were less developed and he states this in his own writings. However, what was developed and original was the combination of philosophy and rhetoric. It was the rhetoric which put the philosophy in motion. Philosophy was the knowledge and rhetoric was the vehicle of use. The two had to be joined to become effective. "The great man was the master of both." (56) His rhetoric and oratorical talents were so outstanding that it too often cast him in that role alone. They were such that he is studied more for oratory and rhetoric than for his ideals of law and principles of government.

Cicero is also described as a "Pre-Christian" when he says, "The <u>mind</u> is the man and not the figure which can be pointed at with the finger. <u>Know, therefore that thou are a divine being, since it is a deity in thee which moves, feels, remembers, foresees, rules, and governs that body, over which it is placed; in the very same way as the Supreme Being governs the world.</u>" (From Cicero's "De Republica" VI 24.) This was written <u>circa 60 B.C.</u> (also quoted in H. Taylor's book, "Cicero - a sketch of his life and works." - see 57-58 p. IX.)

Hannis Taylor (author) puts it succinctly when he says "All that was mortal, of the most gifted son of ancient Italy, went down in the wreck of the Roman Republic, but his <u>immortal</u> part survived as no other human being of his age has survived." (59) This is because, like no other person in ancient history, do we possess anything even remotely resembling his written legacy to posterity. There is still preserved in his own hand, fifty-eight speeches and over nine hundred letters. They touch on all subjects-political, legal, social, and personal; they serve as a mine of accurate information like no other in ancient history from 70 to 43 B.C. (at his death). "He was a man of peace in a world dominated by mob violence and military power." (60)

Today, after 2000 years, his style and form of oratory is not only copied, but is a basic role model as well as to the formation and rhythm of sentence construction. Textbooks on oratory rely heavily on Cicero the Orator, and his speeches are analyzed with clinical exactness by counting the number of nouns, their endings, and sentence structure. The same applies to the length, sequence, and formation of "impact sentences." It has been said that with little doubt, skill in oratory will open the door to success. Success was certainly what Cicero attained. He was a Quaestor, Magistrate, even a "New Man"[1] consul (60a) not to mention Rome's most famous (and feared) orator and lawyer. In this 20th century world, it takes a mental exercise to call to mind another man of history that is equally imposing in our culture today.

His writings demonstrate his sense of good taste and propriety. He states "always, in every part of a speech, as in life, one must consider what is appropriate and befitting." (61) Rhetoric and persuasion became so popular that it became the basis of education in Roman times. The "eloquence of a Senator" is the ideal sought for today in many fields of endeavor. Historians hold two men in highest regard for their oratory: Cicero and Quintillian. Quintillian himself gives Cicero the credit for being the best. He said, "It was Cicero who shed the greatest light on both the practice and theory of oratory. I hardly venture to differ from Cicero." (63) Since the subject of oratory is a text course in itself, it would be informative at this point to provide a brief example. No example of a speech in court cases will be provided here in the interest of brevity. However, one short speech will be given here plus part of a personal letter, as each exemplify his keen perception. These letters, if written today, would still be highly appropriate. Before reading the first letter, it must first be explained that Cicero was selected to be a Quaestor (deputy-governor) of Western Sicily. (Sicily was the granary of Italy, and it was a very important job he performed with his usual

---

[1] Note: A "New Man" was the term given to someone attaining the inner circle of power from outside the usual line of descent or relationship of the ruling hierarchy. It was an exception at that time for a "New Man" to break into the inner circle of consuls.

excellence.) He had been away from Rome for a period of time, was recalled, and this short speech is his experience on his return to Rome in 74 B.C. He had previously been given the honorary title of Patron of Sicily in appreciation of his distinguished services.(63a) The speech is as follows:

"To tell the truth, I really believed at the time that people at Rome were talking about nothing else but my quaestorship. At a time of great scarcity I had sent home an enormous quantity of corn; I had shown myself courteous to the men of business, equitable to the trader, generous to the tax-agents, honest to the provincials, and everyone said that I had been most conscientious in every department of my office. The Sicilians had paid me unheard of honors. So I left Sicily expecting that the Roman people would rush to lay the world at my feet. While I was on my journey home I happened to call in at Puteoli at the height of the season when it was crowded with all the best people. Gentleman, you could have knocked me down with a feather when someone came up to me and asked what day I had left Rome and what was the latest news from Town. I told him that I was on my way back from my province. "Good heavens, yes he said, 'from Africa, isn't it?' I was now pretty fairly annoyed. Not Africa, Sicily, I said. Then some know-it all broke in, 'What, don't you know that our friend here has been quaestor at Syracuse?' I gave up and swallowed my annoyance and turned myself into an ordinary holiday maker. But, gentlemen, I am not sure that incident did not do me more good than if everyone had come up and congratulated me. After I realized that the Roman people were hard of hearing, but their eyes were keen and sharp, I stopped worrying about what people might hear about me and took care that they should see me in the flesh every day. I lived in their sight; I was never out of the Forum." (64)

After reading his speech, one can begin to understand why he is selected as a role model. The next example is a letter to his younger brother Quintus, instructing him on how to govern the province that was entrusted to him (Western Asia).

Instructions on How to Govern:

c. Cicero: Letters to his Brother, - Quintus 1, 8-25 (abridged)
"It is splendid that you have governed Asia for three years without letting a single statue, picture, vase, garment or slave tempt you from the straight and narrow path. Experience by now has taught you that you must answer also for the actions and even the words of your staff. They must not use for the power you delegate to them to maintain their official

position. As for you, let your ears have the reputation of hearing only what they hear, and not slanderous whispers motivated by hope of gain. Let your signet ring be not a mere instrument of another's will, but a guarantee of the firmness of your own. Let the whole province recognize that the welfare, families, reputation and fortunes of all whom you govern are very precious to you, and that you will have nothing to do with either givers or takers of bribes. Let the cornerstones of your administration be, on your part, honesty and self-restraint, on the part of your staff, a sense of honor. Be circumspect but conscientious in your relations with provincials, and with Greeks, should be treated with the respect due those from whom we Romans have learned so much. Keep your servants always firmly in hand. Be strict and impartial in administering justice; grant hearings readily hand down decisions tactfully hear and settle arguments scrupulously. My own opinion is that all who govern others must make their every act contribute to the maximum happiness of those they govern." (66)

This instruction is an example of his views concerning a position of trust and demonstrates his ideals and principles in the matter of governing. Keeping in mind that most of the world outside Rome was ruled by despots, his words stood out in stark contrast. There is little wonder that after him, men aspiring to rise above politics and to be recognized as being a statesman felt content to emulate Cicero.

America's second President, John Adams, felt a keen kinship with Cicero. President Adams' battle with other political forces and his defeat closely paralleled the career of Cicero's, when he also sustained a bitter defeat. In the "Diary of John Adams" he suggests a study of Cicero with reference to the affects of laws on public and private happiness. (66) In Adams' answers to the clerk of court when he was being sworn (in proceedings for practice of law), he states that he reads Latin and that one of the latest books he had read was *Justinian Institutes*[2] with Vinniuss' notes. (a Roman law book) (67)

---

[2]"Institutes" (125 A.D.) A compilation of legal descriptions by Salvius Julianus and his pupil Gaius and were preserved and handed down substantially intact. (P.323 "History of Rome," M. Grant)

Justinian's "Corpus Juris Civilus" (Body of Civil Law) was the codification of all the laws of Rome which became the foundation of modern civil law. (550 A.D.)

Significance: Where John Adams tells of reading "Justinian's Institutes", it is believed he was referring to "Justinian's Code" which included the "Institutes".

Roman law, beginning as a cautious and simple compilation of elementary principles, customs, traditions and law, developed into the most admirable body of jurisprudence ever assembled by man, and was Rome's greatest gift to civilization.

Theories and Principles of Governmental Systems

However interesting he is in the fields of law and rhetoric, Cicero's most important contributions to Western Culture (and to America in particular) are his theories and principles of government. His ideas on "mixed government" are the cornerstone of America's system of "checks and balances" which we point to as the basis of our stable form of government. Beginning with the Constitution, he explains in *DeRepublica* that "The Roman Constitution was not the product or genius of any one man, but of many, and was not evolved in any one lifetime, but in the course of generations and centuries." Cicero was a constitutionalist, a protagonist of those principles, and his influence among the Founding Fathers of America was openly acknowledged by them. They were educated in and were scholars of ancient philosophies. Adams and Jefferson were fluent in Greek and Latin. Jefferson also spoke French and Italian and was said to be a daily reader of Latin works of that era. While they relied upon their knowledge of the ancients, from their most recent past, the influence of English Laws and culture also played a part. However, England was also the recipient of Rome's legacy.

Winston Churchill writes: "For nearly 300 years Britain, reconciled to the Roman system, enjoyed in many respects the happiest, most comfortable, most enlightened times its inhabitants ever had...in culture and learning, Britain was a pale reflection of the Rome scene...There was law, order, there was food, there was warmth and peace, and a long custom of life. Free from barbarism without being sunk into sloth or luxury." (68) Centuries earlier, just as the ancient Italians had stormed their kings demanding protective laws and restraints on their kings and resulting in the XII Tables of Law, so also did the barons of England follow suit against King John of England resulting in the Magna Carta. America also followed similarly with the "Declaration of Independence" from England.

The following quote seems to fairly sum up the forgoing: "The republicanism of Cicero, and of those Romans who thought as he did, was influential in shaping the ideas of the men who founded the American Nation." *Horizon Book of Ancient Rome*, American Heritage, p. 387.

At the time of the formation of American government, the Founding Fathers were not avid followers of English literature. Jefferson read Cicero's "DeSenecute" every year (69) and was committed to the principles of Roman Law. It is clear that the afore mentioned XII Tables of Law and the principles of Natural Law resemble, in substantial form, our own Bill of Rights. "Josia Quincy had three editions of Cicero (one set in twenty volumes) testifying to his devotion to Cicero as a defender of liberty."(70) John Adams, our second president, wrote, "All the ages of the world have not produced a greater statesman than Cicero, his authority should have great weight. His decided opinion in favor of three branches is founded on a reason that is unchallengeable." (71) "Adams' conclusion that liberty depended on separation of powers of government, Legislative, Executive and Judicial, contributed somewhat to give direction to the opinion of the members" (of the Constitutional Convention). (72)

In support of his position in these matters "Adams produced an astonishingly learned and intelligent study of more than forty experiments in democratic governments in the ancient and modern world and analyzed the causes of their failure." (73) They all relied too heavily on a single center of authority and these conclusions were circulated among the delegates to the Constitutional Convention to convince them of the need for a mixed, or Bi-Cameral system of government. (74) John Adams said "The idea of superiority of the mixed system has come down from antiquity," and "the responsibility for mixing the government of the whole with the parts belongs to Cicero." Adams refers us to Cicero's "DeRepublica" 1 #42 (75). C.M. Walsh, author of "The Political Science of John Adams" says, "The evils resulting from failure to establish the balance are much dwelt upon by Adams." (p. 59) The author refers time and again to antiquity, and to Cicero in particular. (75)

The Romans had further split the center of authority by their system of electing two Consuls to share the authority and, "Like our Founding Fathers they trusted no one man". (76) Furthermore, the actions of the Senate could be halted at any time by a Tribune (peoples representative) crying out "Veto." (I forbid)

The sources for the great works of the American Constitution and Bill of Rights are not very difficult to come by. References to this fact are fairly extensive and can be located without great difficulty, but they seem to be overlooked. On December 15, 1991 newspaper editorials were calling our attention to the 200th anniversary of the Bill of Rights. (Two thousand years old would appear to be closer to the mark.) Justice

Douglas (United States Supreme Court, Retired) said, "The Bill of Rights is the greatest Creation of humanity." If this was so, its anniversary should have commanded a little more accuracy.

American Jurisprudence and our system of government was patterned after the system of the Roman Republic.

In 426 A.D. the poet Rutillus Namatianus (of Gaul) wrote concerning Rome: "Spread forth the laws that are to last throughout the ages...Though alone needst not dread the distaffs of the Fates...The span which doth remain...is subject to no bounds...so long as earth shall stand and heaven uphold the stars."

PART III. CHRISTOPHER COLUMBUS

The greatest explorer in history, or the greatest one-man show in history, was Christopher Columbus. His discovery caused the greatest change in world history and this cannot be denied him. There have been numerous attempts at fabricating evidence of colonization of the Western Hemisphere by Norsemen. Some were professionally forged and fabricated. All were thoroughly investigated and revealed to be fakes. In one instance, in the supposedly ancient "Yale University Document," it was found that the ink used on the document had not been put into use until 1920. (77) To their credit, Yale University commissioned the investigation that determined it was fake.

Nevertheless, every anniversary, there are attempts to weaken or discredit the greatest discovery in history. It has now become popular to blame Columbus for the ills and misfortunes that have befallen the Western Hemisphere; from diseases to the ultimate destruction of the rain forests. The ridiculous presumption is that if Columbus had not arrived on the scene, discovering the trade winds "to and from," then none of these misfortunes would have occurred. The Hemisphere would have remained pristine. There are also attempts to take from Christopher Columbus his religion and nationality. Unfortunately for this school of detractors, his religion and nationality are so well established and documented that proponents of this "other nationality" now merely back off with the comment - "Well, it could be, but if he says he's Catholic and Italian we will just have to accept his word. But..." Be that as it may, there is evidence that there were sightings and some landings by Norsemen in the area of Labrador and Newfoundland. Whether by design or by accident, that the Norsemen reached Iceland and Greenland is a well known fact. There is no factual evidence of colonization in the Western Hemisphere by Norsemen (except that which was fabricated and found fake after scientific examination). Nevertheless, even stipulating that Norsemen saw and landed on the coast does not constitute a meaningful discovery. A discovery means more than that. Discovery means the first to gain detailed knowledge of a previously unknown and be able to lay out the route to determine the means of getting there and back again. This Columbus did with such exactness, that within ten years of his discovery there were so many ships "discovering" North America that it prompted Columbus to write, "They all made fun of my plan then; now even tailors wish to discover." (78) One author (not to be identified here) bitterly discredits Columbus' discovery as a mistake of his Catholic Queen. He gives Columbus credit for being lucky and that's all. He says, "if it weren't for Columbus figuring out the trade winds, if it weren't for this and that, etc., etc., he never would have etc., etc." It is certainly well known Columbus did not set out to prove that the earth was round (as is often stated in elementary school books). That the earth was round was speculated and believed by some ancients, including Orientals, 1000 years before Columbus. His goal and plan was to reach the Indies by sailing West. His plan was not based on an idle guess, but on years of study and previously gained experience. He had been sailing for many years to Ireland, down the African Coast and as far out into the Atlantic as the Azores. In fact, after his marriage, he lived in the Canary Islands where he figured out the prevailing winds. "It would be an exaggeration to say that Columbus knew the scientific facts, yet he understood and predicted their effect." (79) He knew exactly what he was doing.

He sailed from Spain, went directly to the Canary Islands where he knew he would pick up the Westerly Trade winds that would lead him to the world's greatest discovery. Returning, he sailed north to the latitude of the Azores to pick up the Easterly Trade Winds that would return him in triumph. He opened wide the doors for further exploration, and with the information he provided, a flood of "discoverers" then went forth.

As a result of his observations and study some of Columbus' discoveries were:

1.   He provided a confirmed knowledge for a route, west and east.
2.   He returned with knowledge of what was to be found and what to expect at the destination. (Recorded and preserved in his journal and logs)
3.   He confirmed the existance of the Trade Winds which were the routes sail boats then used for the next 500 years until the advent of power propelled ships.
4.   He discovered the warm Gulf Stream and its beneficial effect on northern Europe.
5.   He perfected a system of "dead reckoning navigation" in open seas by observing the stars.
* 6.   He discovered the Western magnetic declination of the compass. (72)
7.   He discovered and explored all of Central America on his fourth voyage (Honduras to Panama).

* A momentous navigational discovery that is still in use today throughout the world wherever a compass is used for navigation.

Christopher Columbus was a controversial figure. Some credit him with being a near saint, while others place him at the other end of the spectrum. The consensus lies somewhere in between. He did what he had to do to accomplish his mission. There is no question that he was a poor administrator. However, these aspects of his personality are not the subject of this writing.

If it were not for his characteristics of persistence mixed with intelligence (some say genius), his inquisitiveness and ambition, he may not have succeeded. But isn't that what it takes for those who accomplish the extraordinary? The hero of the world! "Discovery" was his. Attempts to dissect the word "discovery" so as to separate him from it, are last gasps. The history of his 7 years of perseverance, going from one king to another, to secure backing for his voyage is an exciting saga in itself. He was resolute, and religious fervor played a major part in his efforts. "He dreamed of finding gold in such quantities that he could launch an effort to recapture the Holy Land." (81) "He felt empowered on his mission by the Holy Spirit," (82) and he felt that God had chosen him for this mission. There is recorded, in his persistent search for backing for his voyage, the episode of the extent of his demands as payment for his services. His demands were so substantial that they stunned the King of Portugal and also the King and Queen of Spain. On second thought, Queen Isabella agreed. "No discoverer was ever promised so much before his performance. No discoverer's performance so greatly exceeded his promise." (83)

As with so many leading or controversial figures, the differing views depend upon the author. Columbus is described as arriving at the court of Ferdinand and Queen Isabella as "A man in his late thirties with prematurely gray hair that added a touch of nobility to his morose countenance, rode a mule through the western gate of Cordoba on a warmish day in January 1486." (84) He was constantly the center of controversy or disbelief, and part of the reason for this was his failure to fully disclose his plan. He held back his theory of the trade winds because he felt his idea would be stolen. Court jealousies also played a part. The King of Portugal sent a secret voyage to attempt to reach the Indies after talking to Columbus, but the voyage was a failure because Columbus did not disclose his secret of the trade winds. He was again the center of controversy on his later voyages. The problem was mainly his inability to administer the colony that had been established. He was pompous, rash, a dreamer, and dictatorial. The fabrication of records to suit his purposes was not beyond him. He firmly believed that he was sent by God to fulfill this mission and often acted with near fanaticism.

Since there are no paintings of his likeness, we are left with only several descriptions of him. (85) As to his pictorial likeness, the National Geographic (January 1992) shows twelve likenesses by different artists. Controversial to the end, he is triumphant in voyages one and two. He is returned in chains after voyage three. Voyage four is a disaster and he dies in obscurity in 1506. Controversial even in death, four different cities claim he is buried therein. If there was ever one man on whom history pivots, it is Christopher Columbus. "Truly, this uncommon commoner, Christopher Columbus, began a process that, in the words from a passage in one of the books of Esdras, "shook the earth, moved the round world, made the depths shudder and turned creation upside down." (86)

Was this the end of Christopher Columbus? Not really. The next great era of Italian influence on Western Culture was the Italian Renaissance. The beginning of the Modern Age. Many scholars agree that the electrifying event of Columbus' discovery set the Italian Renaissance and the Modern World in fast forward motion.

PART IV. RENAISSANCE

The least controversial fact of the past 2000 years is that the Italian Renaissance ushered in the modern age. On this, virtually every history scholar agrees. Furthermore, there is no question that the force behind it was purely Italian in origin.

The flame of light that was the Roman Empire went out, but there remained, beneath the ashes, embers of its past glory. The past was never completely extinguished. A millennia later, the Italians kicked the ashes, rekindled the flame, and gave birth to a new age. Too often the Renaissance is associated with art alone. This of course is not so. Everything on earth became a matter for study as well as individual expression and exploration. "Renaissance ideals have continued to influence Western thought to the present day." (87)

The subject of the Renaissance, like that of the Roman Empire, occupies a significant library in itself. Its history is not a matter for this writing, but we focus on its over-all influence on Western Culture. The individual accomplishments of the Renaissance, and those that starred in it, are too numerous and well known to repeat here.

The Renaissance that began in Italy in the 1300's spread throughout Europe reaching its peak in the 1500's. Each nation adapted many of the Italian ideas to their own style and taste.

Italy became a mecca for those who had the means to travel and to enjoy the newest and best of everything created by the mind of man. Those unable to go in person read Italian. Anything that was Italian was "in." Everyone that was able seemed to want to savor the Italian experience. Reference to Italy was tantamount to making it acceptable and its backdrop a success. An example of this is Shakespeare. Twelve of his plays had the plot, or its backdrop, in Italy. In every aspect of human endeavor changes were taking place; in the arts, music, literature, political, social, philosophy, religion, architecture, and discovery.

After the momentous discovery by Columbus, in the Renaissance period, discovery was on the agenda of every ruler in the world. The founding of America close on the heels of the Renaissance was a natural recipient of its influence. As stated earlier the Founding Fathers of America, with their close association with England and France, were naturally attracted by this same renewal of civil enlightenment. The Renaissance not only resulted in changes and improvements in human endeavors, it included new thought and art forms entirely. An example of this is the opera. This very complex art form (combining music, singing, scenery, and costume) created for entertainment was exclusively Italian in origin. It quickly spread throughout Europe, then to America, and to all parts of the world. The development of new instruments and harmonics ushered in the modern orchestra.

The Italian influence goes on. The great banking street in London is called Lombard Street, after the Italian money-lenders of Lombardy, Italy. (88) If we, for example, were allowed only one name to offer, we would offer the Universal Renaissance man, Leonardo DaVinci. So far, the world has not produced his equal. He left to posterity 5700 pages of his works. He said, "The natural desire of all good men is knowledge." "Above all, in the lives lived to the fullest by its remarkable men and women, the Italian Renaissance revealed the West's cultural capabilities." (89) Technological improvements aside, virtually every aspect of our modern society has its roots in the Italian Renaissance. (Amazingly, many of our modern technologies are sketched in the papers and records of Leonardo DaVinci.) Professor Paolo E. Taviani said, "Without the Italian Renaissance, there would have been no Modern Age." (90)

However, aside from many individual achievements, Author J.J. Norwich puts it succinctly with a quotation from the book *The Italians, History of Art & Genius of a People*: "Italy conquered Europe through her thinkers and artists, assuming a dominance (reinforced by her explicit claim to be the heir of ancient Rome) from which she has never afterwards been displaced." (91) The Italian Renaissance is not yet a thing of the past. It really refers to a period of revival, a convenient term to describe the great changes that began in that period. Any era that spans centuries, and is transitional, cannot be placed in parenthesis of happening between exact dates. It originally started with art and literature, but then quickly spread to every other endeavor. The excitement of change and discovery fed upon itself stimulating the intelligence and imagination of the Italians, opening a new world of thought and theory. This exciting age of discovery has not yet expired. Since there are no new continents to discover, mankind has looked to the stars. Perhaps while art and literature may have reached a plateau, the age of discovery continues with eyes on outer space. By no means has the book been closed.

PART V. CONTRIBUTING INFLUENCES

In keeping with the theme of Italian influence on Western Culture, there were important contributions brought about by certain individuals that are worthy of individual mention. We are not speaking here of those many well-known names who were prominent in their particular field, but those that pushed forward the movement of modern man on a grander scale. For example: Michelangelo, his genius as an artist, sculptor and architect, has been credited with adding refinement to our culture, but not for changing it. It cannot be said that he changed the course of world history, not-with-standing his peerless talents.

Marco Polo

Marco Polo differs in this respect. Unknowingly, Marco Polo may have added a spark to the tinder that helped to flame the Renaissance and stimulating the ideas of "discovery." Certainly, the concurrence of the dates provide circumstantial evidence to such a possibility. He returned to Italy from Cathay (China) in 1295, with accounts of the highly civilized culture, and brought with him a variety of mementos from firecrackers to spaghetti. This sensational information spread throughout Italy and it must surely have stimulated much activity in other endeavors. Keeping in mind that the Renaissance was said to have begun about 1300, it is highly likely his exploration stimulated others. His book, *Description of the World*, (hand-written and recopied), was the most widely read book in Europe at that time.

Other explorers were attempting to find a sea route to the Indies around Africa, but abandoned their efforts. Sailing south as they approached the equator, it became so hot they turned back believing the sun would destroy the ships' caulking causing them to sink. It was only 150 years later that we find Columbus attempting to get backing for his voyage to reach the Indies. (A comparable time frame of 150 years would be from approximately the Civil War until today.) Historians believe it may have influenced Columbus. (92) There is no official documentation of this, but it certainly seems plausible. Nevertheless, it is another event in the continuous thread of progress toward our Western Culture that continually runs through Italy. This historiography has no counterpart in any other nation of the world.

Petrarch

Another "stepping stone" on the path of Italian influence on Western Culture is Francesco Petraco (1304-74), better known as Petrarch (scholar and philosopher). He is said to have had unmatched influence on world literature. However, that is not the reason for his being selected as a player in this theme. His influence on Western Culture rests on the basis of his scholarship. Historians credit him with being the world's first modern scholar. (93) He roamed the world seeking out the writings of ancient historians and writers such as Livy, Cicero, Josephus, Tacitus, Seneca, Suetonius, Pliny The Younger, and many others.

The writings of these historians might never have been known if he had not searched them out of ancient libraries and old monasteries, translated them and preserved them for reference by future generations of scholars. Therefore, as mentioned previously, he played an important (although indirect) part in the knowledge and development of Western Culture. The great body of historical knowledge provided by his scholarship has also been referred to as a gold mine of information available to the historians and scholars that followed.

An event that occurred a thousand years before the time of Petrarch adds to the significance and importance of his scholarship.

About 330 B.C., Alexander The Great of Greece founded a city in Egypt and named it Alexandria. There he established a library, or more accurately, an archive and deposited there tens of thousands of manuscripts of every kind from all over the known world.

To the great misfortune of future generations, this great archive and its contents was destroyed by mindless barbarian mobs. Over 200,000 manuscripts were lost forever.

The world had to begin again to record its events and history. For the collection, preservation and translation of this later material and for our information and enlightenment, we have Petrarch to thank.

PART VI. LATER INFLUENCES

It has been said that grouping all inventions into categories, they would principally fall into two groups: Communication and Energy. (Medicine was not considered an "invention" but a series of dramatic discoveries by Louis Pasteur of France, discoverer of microbes, and Lister of England, developer of antiseptics. These discoveries changed the course of human development by prevention of disease, alleviation of suffering, and enhancing longevity. In the communication group the two greatest were 1) The printing press with movable type by Johannes Gutenberg of Germany, and 2) The wireless (radio, etc.) by Guglielmo Marconi. Marconi invented a way of sending telegraph signals by wireless radio signals (1895). Previous to his invention, there were theories and experiments in electromagnetic forces, but Marconi's bore successful results. His invention (as did Columbus' discovery) opened the flood-gates to further discoveries, improvements and inventions, and the world of communication has not been the same since. It has been estimated that Americans alone own close to one billion radios. This means of communication has had a significant impact on our personal, social, political and scientific interaction. Its influence was recognized as being so great that it very early came under government regulation and this regulation also extends to private individuals who engage in hobbies involving radio.

The importance of wireless communication is most dramatically demonstrated in our space programs. The messages to and from our astronauts and the control of space crafts millions of miles in space are close to the realm of disbelief. When we consider communication, the control of the Hubble Telescope, and the transmission of pictures from outer space, all occurring in less than 100 years of Marconi's invention, to say his invention opened the flood-gates to modern communication is quite an understatement.

Without the ability to communicate with these instruments of space discovery, there obviously would not have been any in the first place. "Renaissance man's determination to explore his world has its counterpart in today's exploration of outer space." (94) All of this, of course, rested on the ability to communicate by wireless.

Energy (manufactured energy), "the power to do work," is one of mankind's most valued inventive accomplishments.

The amount of power generated to perform work is primarily by electrical energy, and all other methods (sun, wind, tides, gravity, etc.) are virtually nil by comparison. The development of electrical energy required a long and involved process of experiment and discovery. The essential key to the utilization of electrical energy for power required the production of a steady stream of electrical current. Scientists from many countries contributed to the effort, but the key was provided by two scientists joining their separate discoveries. Luigi Galvani (1737-98) of Genoa and Alessandro Volta (1745-1814) (hence "volts") of Rome discovered "the first means of producing a steady current of electricity." *Grolliers Encyc.*, Book E, p. 128. The apparatus utilized for this function is called a "Voltiac Pile."

This breakthrough brought the production of electrical energy to the stage at which we were prior to the coming of Atomic Energy. What the world needed next was an unlimited source of power to generate an unlimited amount of electrical energy.

Enrico Fermi Atomic Energy

It had been known for many years that "splitting the atom" would produce an enormous amount of energy. Efforts to accomplish this had been going on in laboratories and universities all over the world. Scientists with an interest in Nuclear Physics numbered into the hundreds and dated back into the 1800's. Experiments probably numbered in the tens of thousands. It has been said that developing nuclear energy was the greatest scientific project ever attempted. Even greater than the Space Program, which was principally an American effort, nuclear energy was a worldwide effort.

The effort required hundreds of unknown quantities to be ferreted out and hundreds of problems to be solved, some taking years. The success with one mystery often resulted in the appearance of several others. In a simplistic sense, some of the pivotal solutions which needed solving to produce usable power were.

1. Splitting the atom
2. Solving the Fission problem
3. Discovering controlled chain reaction.
4. Invention of the Reactor (Pile) for production of a peacetime source of energy

Because of the complexity of these matters and each one needing a textbook to explain Fermi's work in them, I will list below what scholars and textbooks say of his part in these essential steps.

1. Splitting The Atom (world-wide scientific effort)
"Fermi announced in 1934 what he thought were elements lying beyond uranium, not realizing that he had actually split the atom." (95) Because he did not realize that he had done so, he was not credited as having split the atom although he actually succeeded in doing so. "He proved that slow neutrons are very effective in producing radioactive atoms. This discovery was particularly important because slow neutrons can split U-235." (96)

2. Fission
"Without nuclear fission, neither nuclear weapons nor nuclear electric power plants could have been developed"..."Fermi, together with Leo Szilard, realized fission could cause a chain reaction that would cause a titanic explosion." (97)

3. Chain Reaction
On the Twenty-fifth Anniversary celebration of the first nuclear reactor transmitted over TV from the University of Chicago, December 2, 1967, President Lyndon Johnson said, "More than any other person, this anniversary observance honors the great Italian physicist, Enrico Fermi, for it was the scientists under his direction who accomplished the event we are celebrating today, the first controlled release of energy from the nucleus of the Atom. Enrico Fermi's experiment opened up a new world of matter and energy... In Chicago, 25 years ago, Enrico Fermi and his fellow scientist, in a single stroke, increased man's available energy more than a thousandfold. They placed in our hands the power of the Universe itself." (98) Dr. Arthur Compton, in a phone call to his colleague Dr. Conant at Harvard, announced the secret experimental success in a cryptic message: "The Italian navigator has just landed in the new world. The natives are friendly." (99)

At the University of Chicago, there is a plaque on the wall where his successful experiments took place. It states:

"On December 2, 1942, man achieved here the first self-sustaining chain reaction and thereby initiated the controlled release of nuclear energy."

4. <u>Nuclear Reactor (Piles)</u>

A device that produces a vast amount of energy, sometime called an Atomic Reactor or an Atomic Pile. "Enrico Fermi designed an apparatus which he called an Atomic Pile." (100) "He built the first Atomic Pile." (101) The obvious importance of controlled reaction is Fission, under control, allows nuclear energy to be produced for peaceful purposes. If it becomes uncontrolled, it produces an atomic explosion.

Here again, with the discoveries by Dr. Fermi, we have a reenactment of the Italian Legacy. There is law, Columbus, Rennaissance, Marconi and now the new age of endless energy.

<u>Explosives</u> - Nitroglycerine is an extremely powerful liquid explosive. Its useful and widespread use has changed the face of the earth. Mountains have been leveled or tunneled and canals and river courses built or changed. (For example, the recently completed tunnel from England to France under the English Channel) It was discovered by Ascanio Sobrero, a chemist in Milan, Italy in 1847. It was extermely dangerous to handle as merely shaking it caused it to explode. Alfred Nobel, in the 1860's combined it with a clay-like substance called Kieslgubr that made it safer to handle without reducing its power. He named it dynamite. Nobel invented and patented a detonator cap and it has since been used universally in every kind of explosive until the advent of atomic energy.

Enrico Fermi's Other Awards & Recognitions

1. Received the United States Congressional Medal of Merit.
2. Elected to the Royal Society of London (England's oldest scientific society).
3. Element #100 "Fermium" was named after him. (102)
4. Recognized for developing the mathematical statistics required to clarify a large class of sub-atomic phenomena.
5. Recognized for discovering neutron-induced radioactivity.
6. Recognized for the first and only theory on beta decay. "It was so complete that its description of the phenomenon has remained essentially unchanged to this day." (103)
7. Establishment of Enrico Fermi Award (He was also its first recipient).
8. Nobel Prize (while still in Italy). (104) Awarded this even before his more sensational work and discoveries in America.

The Atomic Age has many fathers, but the grandfather of them all appears to be Enrico Fermi. In the book *Fermi-The Man and His Theories* by Pierre deLatil (in France) translated by Len Ortzen, he comments of Fermi... "He was the most brilliant among the galaxy of scientists working at Los Alamos."--- "The man who freed nuclear energy was an Italian."

--- "A man with such an all-embracing mind inevitably recalls the great men of the Renaissance, so many of them were Italian too."-- "How can one not help feeling that the man who experienced this great adventure is one of the foremost heroes in the history of mankind." (105)

Further Reading - *Enrico, The Man & His Theories; Fermi* (Towson State Library) [QC774 F4L. 37131] Translated from French, by P. DeLatil-Ryerson Press- Toronto-1964.

PART VII. OTHER INFLUENCES

There were many other Italian participants spreading the enlightenment that was already underway. Their contributions were in a sense, not original to the point of bringing about a new era or a new age, but nevertheless, important enough in their parallel direction.

Niccolo Machiavelli (1496-1527)

Popular theories on politics in the world today are very often patterned after his philosophies on the subject. He is often referred to as the father of modern politics and probably the first political analyst. Although he was very controversial, most scholars agree that he was a keen observer of the political scene. His books and discourses are still subjected to divergent interpretation of his motives and views, and he is more or less credited with originating a new science (political science). This science, concerning the policies and aims of government, has gradually escalated into a function of prime importance. "Machiavelli may well be the most political of all great political theorists." (106) - (107)

The Other "Discoveries"

As Columbus said, "They all made fun of my plan then; now even tailors wish to discover." (108) Almost every other European nation launched ships making discoveries all over the world. Prominent among the admirals of those nations were Italians. They kept the age of discoveries very much alive gathering knowledge of other lands and new routes, thus opening up world trade.

John Cabot (1450? - 1498?)

His birth name was Giovanni Caboto. Although he was born in Genoa, Italy, he sailed for England. He is given credit for landing in North America, claiming the land for England, in 1497. The area was believed to be Newfoundland.

Giovanni DeVerrazano (1485-1528) Italian

Sailed for France. He explored the east coast of North America and was the first European to sight New York Harbor and Narragansett Bay. He was also the first to name new discoveries after places and persons in the old world. While exploring in the Caribbean he went ashore, in what is now Guadeloupe, was killed and eaten by cannibals. One of the longest suspension bridges in the world is named in his honor, the Verrazano Bridge in New York Harbor. The center span alone is 4,260 feet long and has six lanes on a double deck.

Amerigo Vespucci (1454-1517) Italian

Explorer for whom America is named. He made extensive explorations to the American mainland and was recognized as an experienced navigator and map maker. His letters claimed that he had discovered a new continent in 1497; the first explorer to declare that this was a new continent. As Columbus did, Vespucci sailed for Spain.

The Calendar

Every day in the year is an "Italian connection." Our lives revolve around dates. Almost every event of our lives has a date attached to it. In fact, the effective date of an event has become almost of equal importance as the event itself. Everything in our lives seems to depend on a date on the Calendar. We are born, live and die, by dates.

The actual solar year is 365 days, 5 hour, 48 minutes and 46 seconds. Ancient calendars, dating back to the Egyptians, Mayans and Hebrews did the best they could, but were never exact enough. After hundreds of years, their calendars were off, resulting in a mixture of seasons. Julius Caesar, a man who knew what he wanted and had the power to grasp it, developed the Julian Calendar in 46 B.C. (They of course did not know it was "B.C.") They worked out a Calendar year that was 365 1/4 days and was in use for 1500 years. However, even the great Caesar was in error by 11 minutes and 14 seconds over the course of a year. Therefore, over time, (150 years) even that small difference added up to over 10 days. Easter fell earlier than it should and Pope Gregory XIII corrected this. How, is not important here, as this discourse is not intended to be a thesis on the development of the Calendar. The bottom line is that his calendar (adjusted to the Julian Calendar) is now accurate to 1/2 second in 100 years.

Virtually every nation on earth now uses a calendar initiated by Rome. (109)-(110) The Influence on Western Culture continues.

The names of the months:

January is named after the Roman god Janus, a two-faced god with one face looking forward and the other looking back. He was worshiped as a god of beginnings.
February is derived from the Roman feast of purification held in the second month of the year. (februa, Latin for purification)
March is named after Mars, the all-powerful Roman god of war.
April is named after the Latin word Aprilis and refers to "opens" for growth.
May is named after the Roman goddess of growth, Maia.
June is named after the Roman goddess Juno, goddess of marriage. (the month of good fortune for brides)
July is named after Julius Caesar.
August is named after Agustus Caesar.
September is named after the Latin number seven. (septem)
October is named for the Latin number eight, (octo) prior to the rearrangement.
November is named after nine. (novem)
December is named after Latin ten. (decem)

The older Roman Calendar had ten months, but two months were added at the beginning. This change pushed forward the numbered months which were retained under the new calendar. (Julius and his nephew, Agustus, named two for themselves.)

Language

While our language is "English", over 50% of the words are rooted in Latin. Rome invaded England about 50 B.C. and stayed for about 400 years. They of course brought their language and named the country "Britannia." Much later, around the year 1066, when the Anglo-Saxons conquered England, they also brought changes in the language. But, the language of the Anglo-Saxon tribes was heavily based in Latin. The extent of Latin throughout the world can be appreciated when one considers that English is spoken by more people than any other, except Chinese. "Rome has passed away; the language of Rome still remains to enrich the intellectual life of mankind." (111)

A brief review of a Latin vocabulary text will list hundreds of words spelled almost exactly the same in Latin as in English, with perhaps only the addition of an "m" or "um."

The following Latin words (selected at random are spelled exactly the same in English: actor, alumnus, aqua, assensor, animal, appendix, arbor, arbiter, area, audio, basis, bonus, benign, campus, capital, censor, census, condominium, conductor, conqueror, consensus, debit, doctor, dormitory, duplex, elastic, equilibrium, favor, formula, genius, idea, ignoramus, imperium, index, incongruous, interpreter, labor, legislator, locus, maximum, minus, moderator, momentum, multiflex, negative, neuter, nucleus, odium, omen, plus, promisor, radius, ratio, referendum, republica, rumor, senator, severe, status, stadium, successor, superior, suspicious, tenor, testator, ultimatum, uterus, vacuum, valor, versus, veto.

ITALIAN - ENGLISH

The following list provides an interesting similarity between some Italian and English words. Some, with very slight difference in spelling, correspond to the same word in English. The list that follows are a few examples due to space limitation:

a. Italian words which are spelled exactly like corresponding English words except that they have an additional vowel sound (a, o or e) at the end.

poeta	probelma	artista	forma	lista	persona
poet	problem	artist	form	list	person
pianista	musica	concerto	moderno	evento	periodo
pianist	music	concert	modern	event	period
spirito	calmo	monumento	porto	colore	civile
spirit	calm	monument	port	color	civil
cordiale	cereale	classe	generale	regione	importante
cordial	cereal	class	general	region	important

b. Italian words which have a vowel sound where the corresponding English word has a final silent "e."

rosa	guida	data	statura	vaso	uso	sincero
rose	guide	date	stature	vase	use	sincere
fortunato	stato					
fortunate	state					

c. Italian words differing more or less in spelling from corresponding English words, but whose meaning is easily guessed.

appartamento	articolo	scuola	generoso	teatro	famoso
apartment	article	school	generous	theatre	famous
famiglia	programma	letteratura	edificio	centro	turista	attore
family	program	literature	edifice	centre	tourist	actor
dottore	gruppo	scultura			
doctor	group	sculpture			

d. Words in which the Italian ending "-zione" equals the English "-tion".

conversazione	emozione	stazione	informazione	competizione
conversation	emotion	station	information	competition

disposizione
disposition

e. Words in which the Italian ending a or ia equals the English ending "y".

popolarita	opportunita	quantita	qualita	citta	dignita
popularity	opportunity	quantity	quality	city	dignity

formalita	gloria	varieta	activita	identita	velvocita
formality	glory	variety	activity	identity	velocity

commedia	geografia	societa	facilita
comedy	geography	society	facility

f. Some musical and culinary words borrowed directly from the Italian, often with only slight changes in pronunciation.

sonata	soprana	contralto	alto	opera	primadonna
fortissimo	pianissimo	spaghetti	maccheroni	raviolo	solo aria
minestrone	antipasto	spumone	madrigal	piano	

g. Some of the many verbs which differ from corresponding English verbs only in the matter of ending.

visitare	conversare	presentare	arrivare	confessare
to visit	to converse	to present	to arrive	to confess

decidere	preferire	studiare	indicare	preparare
to decide	to prefer	to study	to indicate	to prepare

informare	costare	dividere	differire
to inform	to cost	to divide	to differ

(112)

As previously mentioned, while some Italian influences did not change history, there were many that provided substantial contributions to Western Culture.

The following passage is "reprinted with permission of ANTHENEUM PUBLISHERS, AN IMPRINT OF MACMILLAN PUBLISHING COMPANY, FROM "THE ITALIANS" BY LUIGI BARZINI, COPYRIGHT 1964, ALL RIGHTS RESERVED." (Their permission is acknowledged and appreciated.)

Italy's smaller contributions to everyday life are so numerous as to go unnoticed. There would be no pistols but for the city of Pistoia; no savon in France, but for the city of Savona; no faience anywhere but for the city of Faenza; no millinery but for the city of Milan; no blue jeans but for the city of Genoa, Genes, where the blue cotton cloth was first produced, and no Genoa jibs; no Neapolitan ice-cream, no Roman candles, no Venetian blinds, no Bologna sausages, no Parmesan cheese, no Leghorn hens. Italians have discovered America for the American; taught poetry, statesmanship, and the ruses of trade to the English; military art to the Germans; cuisine to the French; acting and ballet dancing to the Russians; and music to everybody. If some day this world of ours should be turned into a cloud of radioactive dust in space, it will be by nuclear contrivances developed with the decisive aid of Italian scientists.

The list of the famous Italians is awe-inspiring. It is well to record them here, as they will scarcely be mentioned in the rest of the book, written with the presumption that the reader is well acquainted with them. Here are some of the main ones: The saints: Saint Francis, Santa Catarina da Siena, San Bernardino da Siena, San luigi Gonzaga, Saint Thomas of Aquino. The sinners: the Borgia family (Spanish but acclimatized), Cellini, Caravaggio, Cagliostro, Casanova. The political thinkers: Dante Alighieri, King Frederick of Hohenstaufen of the two Sicilies (born in Italy, the inventor of the modern state, the state as a work of art). Machiavelli, Guicciardini, Mazzini, Cavour. The military leaders: Giovanni dalle Bande Nere, Raimondo Montecuccoli (who led Austrian armies), Napoleon, Garibaldi. The admirals: Andrea Doria, Mocenigo, Morosini, Bragadin, Caracciolo. The scientists: Galileo Galilei, Leonardo da Vinci, Volta, Marconi, Fermi. The navigators: Columbus, Vespucci, the Cabots. The thinkers: Saint Thomas of Aquino, Campanella, Croce, Vico. The poets: Dante Alighieri, Boccaccio, Petrarch, Leopardi, Manzoni. The sculptors: Verrocchio, Donatello, Ghiberti, della Robbia, Cellini, Michelangelo, Bernini. The painters: Giotto, Botticelli, Fra Angelico, Leonardo da Vinci, Piero de la Francesca, Perugino, Michelangelo, Raphael, Titian, Tintoretto, Tiepolo, Modigliani. The musicians: Palestrina, Pergolesi, Monteverdi, Vivaldi, Rossini, Verdi Bellini, Donizetti, Puccini, Toscanini.

These are, of course, names of the first magnitude. <u>The second and third category</u> could easily fill a small city's telephone book!

END OF BOOK I

EPILOGUE AND SUBJECTS FOR FURTHER STUDY

As mentioned earlier, there are many other topics that did not meet the criteria for initiating world changes but were nevertheless influential to our customs, personal lives, and government. The following, with brief notation, are not in any particular order of importance, but did exert influences. <u>Builders</u> - That the Romans were builders, there is no dispute. They invented cement and perfected construction of the arch and dome. Some of the greatest ruins of antiquity are not in Rome, but are in Spain, France, England, Greece, Switzerland, Asia Minor, Syria and North Africa. They did things in a big way. Three of the largest blocks of stone known to have been used in any structure in the world, over 1000 tons each, were used in the temple of the Sun in Baalbec, Syria. *Early European History*. H. Webster-D.C. Heath Co. Boston, 1917. p. 217.

<u>Army</u> - The near invincibility of the Roman army has been legend. They laid the ground work for creating an established army system that exists to modern times. Instead of forming an army of pick-ups off the farm, when needed, and required to bring their own sword, the Romans established a permanent force and provided the armaments.

1. They required a solemn oath.
2. Required submission to their commanders with severe penalties for infractions.
3. Desertion was severely punished.
4. In time of war, they instituted the Draft.
5. The Empire paid for their clothes and arms.

They were professionals. Sworn to die for the Empire and often defeated opponents with much larger forces than their own. *The Rise and Fall of the Roman Empire*, Gibbon-Viking Press, N.Y., p. 37 Abridged version-Penguin Books. In 216 B.C. Hannibal defeated an experienced Roman Army in a bitter battle at Cannae, and after his victory, not one defeated city became his ally, which was often the practice. Such was the loyalty of the population to the Roman ideology. (113)

<u>Death Penalty</u> - The death penalty had, for all intents and purposes, been abolished for free-born citizens. (Not so for captives in war, nor for common criminals such as cutthroats and highwaymen.) The Senate had no power to order the death even of a conspirator, they were usually exiled. *Cicero, A Political Biography*, David Stockton, Oxford University Press, London-1971 - p. 136 & 137.

<u>Marriage & Position of Women</u> - Wedding customs of Greeks and Romans were similar in regard to certain ceremonies and customs, but there was a difference however in the position of a woman in marriage. Athenian women were held virtually in bondage. Permission was required to go out, she took no part in banquets, entertainments or social functions of her husband, and she lived a life of confinement. Married women in Rome, while under the "guardianship" of a husband or a male protector (if a widow), enjoyed freedom and liberality under Roman Law. She could mingle freely in society and was a friend and confidante of her husband, as well as the housekeeper. She could own property in her own name and buy and sell objects of value. *Early European History*, Classical Civilization, H. Webster, D.C. Heath Co.-Boston-1917 p. 257).

Property rights came gradually to women of the western non-Roman world and it was not until the Nineteenth Century that they became generally accepted.

Roman liberality was far ahead of it's time, as cited in the following examples:

1. Under Common Law (of England and later adopted by the U.S. in 1789) a wife's inherited real property became the property of her husband upon marriage, and he could dispose of it during his lifetime without her consent. Her property was liable for his debts, and her rents and profits belonged to him (see *Real Property* by Tiffany. p. 322, Sec 309) (law school text book)

2. Socially, Roman women sat in chairs with their guests, or reclined like men at dinner. (Elsewhere in the world women were excluded from social functions and kept out of sight of the guests.)
   The following is a passage in *Greece & Rome* (a Nat. Geo. Book Service) concerning Roman women during a social feast. Trimalchi (in Petronius' *Statyricon*) is reported to have told his wife, "chat with the guests and keep an eye on the silver." He said, "she has the eyes and claws of a hawk."

3. Many Roman women "lived hard and in the fast lane" (*History of Rome*, Michael Grant).

4. Roman women were allowed to seek divorce, but divorce was easier to obtain by a man.

5. Women exerted great political influence over those in positions of power.

6. Two women, Messalina and Agrippina, rose to the title of Empress of the Empire, and both ruled as de facto "Emperors', but were not historically recorded as such. However, it was recognized by the population that they were, in fact, the rulers.

   Messalina was the wife of the mentally slow Emperor, Claudius (41 to 54 AD). She was described (by historian Tacitus) as "beautiful, capricious, gay, powerful, reckless, and avid of luxury and money." The record of her administration was exceedingly poor. *The Women of Caesar* by Guglielmo Ferrero-Barns & Noble, N.Y. 1993, pp. 154-186.

   Agrippina was the mother of Nero who became the Emperor in his youth (54-68 AD). Agrippina, as Empress, ruled the Empire until his majority. She was known as an "excellent administrator, frugal and careful of all items of income and expense." Her administration was described as "rigid as if it were a man's," and it was referred to as the government of Agrippina. [Ibid pp. 205-06]

7. After the assassination of Caesar, it was the mother of Brutus who called a conference (not the Senate) to decide what should be done next. *History of Rome*, Michael Grant, p. 243.

8. It was Emperor Constantine who in 330 A.D. declared his mother Empress of the Roman Empire.

Note - The carrying of the bride over the threshold into the house was a Roman custom. (If the bride while walking in herself should stumble, it was considered a bad omen.) *Greece & Rome*, A National Geographic Book Service, Washington, D.C. 1960, p. 363.

Education - The Romans were the first people to make the learning of oratory and a foreign language an essential part of education. In 200 B.C. the study of Greek was a requirement as basic education. *Early European History*, Classical Civilization, By H. Webster, D.C. Heath Co., Boston 1917 p. 256 *Colliers Encyclopedia*, Classic Education, p. 602.

Feast of Thanksgiving - This feast was the custom in Rome from about 60 B.C.

Table Etiquette - The wife of the Doge Domenice Silvie of Venice in 1100 A.D. introduced forks to tableware, rather than eating with hands or stabbing food with the knife that everyone carried. The fork was two-pronged and became widely used during the Renaissance. They were introduced into France and England as a result of the Renaissance about 1650 and were first brought to America by Governor John Winthrop of Massachusetts in 1630. *World Book Encyclopedia*, Chicago, 1982, Volume II

Tourism - Surprisingly, Italy had a great deal to do with the development of tourism. Around the close of the Renaissance period, people of Europe began traveling to Italy to experience the richness of the culture that they had heard about. Also, around the same time, Giovanni Batista Piranesi (1770-1778), artist, architect, and archeologist created over 1300 etchings of the awe-inspiring wonders of Roman antiquity. He made thousands of prints from these etchings and went about Europe selling them and stirring up great interest in Roman archaeology. The things that people had heard about Rome, coupled with the pictorial descriptions, had the same affect as today's travel agents. In the 1800's people flocked to Italy. Guide books and itineraries were provided even then. It has never subsided. In 1990, over 50 million tourists visited Italy. (A number nearly equal to the entire population.) No nation in the world has as many visitors as Italy. *The Italians*, David Willey, B.B.C. London, 1984 *Colliers Encyclopedia*, Roman Archaeology, p.601.

A study of world history is a study of the Italians. A small nation, its people large in vitality, intelligence, and initiative, have time and again risen to lead the way to a new era. The Italians were in the mainstream throughout. It is hard to imagine the world without Rome, Cicero, Columbus, and the Renaissance.

FURTHER STUDY
(RECOMMENDED SOURCES)

For those interested in further study I recommend the following:

1. A subscription to the *Italian Journal* is a must. An excellent source of economic and cultural information on all phases of Italian subjects.

   Write to: The Italian Academy Foundation Inc.

   Italian Journal

   Victor Tesoro, Editor & Publisher

   278 Clinton Avenue

   Dobbs Ferry, NY 10522

If you are currently receiving temporary sample issues, confirm with $36.00 annual paid subscription. It's the best.

2. *Roman Civilization*, Volume I, By M. Reinhold. Columbia University Press - (Out of print - in libraries only)

3. *The History of the Roman Empire*, Prentice-Hall.

4. *Decline and Fall of the Roman Empire*, Gibbon.

5. *The Political Science of John Adams* (A study in the theory of mixed government) C.H. Walsh.

6. *Letters of Cicero*, L.P. Wilkinson Ed.

7. *Rethoric at Rome*, H.L. Clarke.

8. *This was Cicero*, H.J. Haskel.

9. *Columbus-The Great Adventure*, P.E. Taviani. (World's foremost scholar on Columbus) Also very entertaining.

10. *The Renaissance, Maker of Modern Man*, A National Geographic Book Service- 1972

11. *Fermi, the Man and His Theories*, Translated from French (At Towson State University Library only) A must!

12. *Italian Heroes of American History*, Louis A. Lepis. Published by: Americans of Italian Descent, Inc. - Suite 1605, 299 Broadway, NY 10007. Excellent reference for later period of Italians farther than those in this treatise.

Further study is suggested with reference to <u>Philip Mazzei,</u> an ardent supporter of the American Revolution and close friend of Thomas Jefferson. He wrote many articles and books supporting the aims of the new America, and lived with Jefferson for a while at Monticello, and became his business associate. Mazzei detailed his theories to Jefferson concerning the essentials needed to form a reliable representative form of government for the new nation. They were both interested in horticulture and Mazzei invented several machines for agricultural improvement. In recognition and appreciation of Mazzei's support and his contributions in helping to form the new nation, the United States honored him in 1980 by publication of a postage stamp. ($0.40 airmail) *Encyclopedia Britannica*, and *Thomas Jefferson, The Man, His World, and His Influence*, L. Weymouth

<u>William Paca</u> - We Baltimoreans are familiar with William Paca (Paca Street and Paca House) A signer of the Declaration of Independence, William Paca was known for his fervent desire for American Independence and his patriotism. It is appropriate to note here that in the history of America, no Italian has ever been accused of being a traitor or spy. (Most libraries)

<u>Peter Amadeo Giannine</u> - Provided the greatest change in banking in the United States. Founded the Bank of America in California, which became the largest bank in the world, and was a major pioneer of branch banking. (Most libraries.)

I

BIBLIOGRAPHY AND REFERENCES - BOOK I

(1) *The Italians, History, Art, and the Genius of a People*, J.J. Norwich, editor - Portland House, N.Y. 1983 - p. 31

(2) *The Italians - Rome and the Empire*, Text by Karl Chris Portland House, NY. 1983 - p. 41

(3) *Decline and Fall Of the Roman Empire*, Gibbon, Viking Press, Inc. N.Y. (Penguin Group) 1952 p. 690. (Abridged)

(3a) *History of Civilization*, Part III. Will Durant Simon & Schuster, N.Y. 1944 p. VII

(4) *Black's Law Dictionary*, West Publishing Co. St. Paul, Min. 1933 3rd Ed.

(5) *Bouvier's Law Dictionary*, (Unabridged) Rawle's Edition. West Publishing Co. 3rd Edition - 1914

(6) *The History of the Roman Empire*, Prentice Hall - 509 to 287 B.C. 1962 & 1984 Chap. 5 - p. 57

(7) *World History*, Wright & Stampp, Editors, McGraw-Hill, N.Y. 1914 p. 64

(8) *World History*, (Above) p. 64

(9) *Greece & Rome*, National Geographic Books, Builders of Our World Quest for Our Golden Heritage, - 1968, p. 26 (Merle Severy)

(10) *Imperial Rome*, (Great Ages of Man-A History of World Cultures) Time-Life Books, N.Y. 1965 p. 7

(11) Void

(12) Void

(13) Gibbon, *Decline and Fall of the Roman Empire*, (#3 above) p. 27 (Abridged)

(14) *The Island Race*, Winston Churchill, Alexis Gregory, ED. NY 1971 p. 202

(15) *Italian Journal*, 1991 #5 & 6 Vol. V - The Legacy of Rome and the U.S., Prof. R. Dizenzo, Loyola UN Chicago. p. 48

(16) *World History*, McGraw & Hill, N.Y. Wright & Stampp, ED 1964 p. 73

(17) *Ancient Rome*, C. Flagg, Warwick Press, N.Y. 1979, p. 21-22

(18) *An American History*, D.S. Muzzey. Ginn & Co. Boston 1911 pp. 156-157

(19) *Early European History*, H. Webster, D.C. Heath Co. Boston 1917 p. 217

(20) *Imperial Rome*, (Great Ages of Man) - A History of World Cultures-Time-Life Books, N.Y. 1965 p. 14

(21) *Imperial Rome*, Ibid p. 13

(22) Ibid (21)-pp. 13-14

(23) Ibid (21) p. 13

(24) Ibid (20) p. 14

(25) *Decline and Fall of the Roman Empire*, Gibbon, Viking Press, N.Y. Penguin Group 1952 p. 67 (Abridged)

(26) *Imperial Rome*, Ibid (20) p. 11

(27) *World History*, Wright & Stampp, ED. McGraw & Hill, N.Y. 1964 p. 70

(28) *Decline and Fall of the Roman Empire*, Gibbon, Viking Press, Inc. N.Y. Penguin Group-1952 - p. 55 (Abridged)

(29) Ibid (28) p. 50 (Abridged)

(30) Ibid (29) p. 53 (Abridged)

(31) Ibid (30) p. 54 (Abridged)

(32) *The Idea of Rome*, David Thompson. Ed. Albuquerque, UN. of Mexico Press. 1971 p. XI

(33) Ibid (32) p. XII

(34) Ibid (33) p. XIII

(35) *The Roman Mind At Work*, Paul Mackendrick, D. Van Nostrand Co., Princeton, N.J. 1958 R.C.

(36) *Black's Law Dictionary*, 3rd Ed. West Publishing Co., St. Paul, Minn.

(37) *Encyclopedia Britannica*, Vol. 12, (Ready Ref. Edition)

(38) *Early European History*, Webster-D.C. Heath, Boston, 1917. p. 207

(39) *Roman Civilazation*, Vol. I, M. Reinhold, Columbia University Press, N.Y. 1951 p. 105 to 115 (Reprint Edition)

(40) *Encyclopedia Britannica*, Vol. #3, p. 333 & 338 "Civil Law" 15th Edition

(41) See (38) *Early European History*, Webster, D.C. Heath-Boston, 1917 p. 207

(42) *Eerdman's Handbook of Christianity*, Lion Publishing Co., Heart-fordshire, England - 1977. p. 63 (St. Paul)

Italian Journal - "The Legacy of Rome & The U.S. Prof. R. Dizenzo 1991 #5 & 6 Vol. V - p. 49 (Published by Italian Academy Foundation, Inc. N.Y., Victor Tesoro, Founder)

(43) *Encyclopedia Britannica*, Vol. #3 - p. 333 & 338 "Civil Law" 15th Edition

(44) *The History of the Roman Empire*, Chap. 5 (509 to 287 B.C.) Prentice Hall, N.J. 1962 & 1984 - p. 58

(45) *Early European History*, Webster, D.C. Heath, Boston 1917 p. 151

(46) *Roman Civilization*, M. Reinhold, Columbia University Press, N.Y. 1951 - p. 102 (Vol. I of Original Edition)

The Story of Civilization, Will Durant, Simon & Shuster, N.Y. Part III -p. 23

(47) *The Romans*, Silver & Burdet Co. 1985 Morristown, N.J. p. 53

(48) *The Law & Life of Rome*, J.A. Crook, Cornell UN. Press, N.Y. 1984 - p. 212

(49) *Italian Journal* - "The Legacy of Rome & The U.S." Prof. R. Dizenzo 1991 # 5 & 6, Vol. V - p. 49 (Published by Italian Academy Foundation, Inc. N.Y., Victor Tesoro, Founder)

(50) *A Literary History of Rome*, 2nd Ed., J.W. Duff, London 1920 -p. 351

(51) *The Roman Way*, Edith Hamilton, W.W. Norton, N.Y. 1932 - p. 61

(52) *The Course of Civilization*, Vol. II, Strayer, Gatzke, Harrison, Harcourt, Brace & World, Inc. N.Y. 1962 - p. 57

(53) *Black's Law Dictionary*, West Publishing Co., St. Paul, Minn. 1933 3rd Edition

(54) *Cicero in America*, Italian Journal 1991 #3 & 4 Vol. V.   Italian Academy Foundation, N.Y. p. 26

(55) *Cicero - A Sketch of His Life & Works*, H. Taylor, A.C. McClurg Co. Chicago 1918 2nd Edition pp. 72 & 73

(56) *World Book Encyclopedia*, 1982 - "Cicero" p. 114

(57) *Cicero - A Sketch of His Life & Works*, H. Taylor, A.C. McClurg Co. Chicago 1918 2nd Edition pp. 72-73 & p. IX

(58) Ibid p. IX

(59) Ibid p. IX

(60) *World History*, Wright & Stampp, McGraw-Hill, N.Y. 1964 p. 69

(60a) *History of Rome*, Michael Grant, 1914 p. 199

(61) *Rhetoric At Rome*, M.L. Clarke, Cohen & West, London, 1962 p. 82

(62) Void

(63) *Rhetoric At Rome*, M.L. Clarke, Cohen & West, London, 1962 p. 110

(64a) *Letters Of Cicero*, L.P. Wilkinson, Hutchinson UN. Press, London, Original Edition 1949

A Political Biography, David Stocton, Oxford UN. Press, London -1971 p. 14

(64) *A Political Biography*, David Stocton, Oxford UN. Press, London -1971 p. 14 - 15

(65) *The Roman Mind At Work*, Paul MacKendrick, D. Van Nostrand Co., Princeton, N.J. 1958 - pp. 109-110

(66) *Diary & Autobiography*, John Adams, L.H. Butterfield, Editor - Vol I - Period 1755 to 1770. (1759) The Becknap Press of Harvard UN. Cambridge, Mass. 1961 p. 73

(67) Ibid - Vol III - p. 273

(68) *The Birth of Britain*, Winston Churchill, Dodd-Mead & Co, N.Y. 1956 -pp. 35- 36

(69) *This Was Cicero*, H.J. Haskel - A.A. Knopf Inc. N.Y. 1942, Chap. II " A Roman Visits 18th Century London"

(70) Ibid

(71) Ibid

(72) Ibid

(73) Ibid

(74) *The Political Science of John Adams*, (A Study in the Theory of Mixed Government) C.M. Walsh - Books for Libraries Press, N.Y. 1969 - p. 25 (in notes)
Also - *Cicero's DeRepublica* (i 45, 54, 59, 61 i 41, 65)
Also - *Polybius* - vi 3 - 18
Also - *Dionasis of Halicarnasis* - ii Parag. 7 vii 55

(75) Ibid

(76) *Greece & Rome*, A National Geographic Book "Quest For Our Golden Heritage" by Merle Severy 1971 - p. 26

(77) *Columbus, The Great Adventure*, P.E. Taviani Orion Books, N.Y. 1989 - p. 26

(78) *Encyclopedia Britannica*, 1989 Ed. (The Detailed Study Book)

(79) Ibid (69) - p. 41

(80) Ibid (69) - p. 45 & 65

(81) Ibid (69) - p. 255

(82) *National Geographic Magazine* - Jan. 1992 - p. 39

(83) Ibid (70) - p. 692

(84) *Isabella of Spain*, W.T. Walsh - Tan Books - 1930 - p. 290

(85) Ibid (69) - p. 252
National Geographic Magazine (Jan. 1992) p. 17

(86) *National Geographic Magazine* (Jan. 1992) p. 39

(87) *World Book*, World Book, Inc. Chicago - 1982 - p. 224d

(88) *Horizon Book of Renaissance*, American Heritage Pub., N.Y. 1961 p. 15

(89) *The Renaissance Maker of Modern Man*, National Geographic Book, Washington, D.C. 1972 - M. Severy, Ed. 1972 - p. 7

(90) *Columbus - The Great Adventure*, P.E. Taviani - Orion Books - N.Y. 1989 - p. 263

(91) *The Italians - History, Art, & Genius of a People*, J.J. Norwich, Portland House, N.Y. 1983 - p. 104

(92) Ibid (79) - p. 573

(93)   *Early European History*, By H. Webster. D.C. Heath Co., Boston,
       -1917 - p. 592

(94)   Ibid - (79) - p. 224d

(95)   *World Book Encyclopedia*, Chicago 1982 - "F" - p. 77

(96)   Ibid

(97)   *Interactions*, Sheldon Glashow - Warner Books - N.Y. - p. 14

(98)   *Nuclear Milestones*, Glen Seaburg - W.H. Freeman Co. San Francisco 1972 - pp.
       31 - 32

(99)   *The Atom & Nucleus*, Geo. Gamow - Prentice Hall, NY 1961 - p. 123

(100) *Encyclopedia Britanica*, 15th Edition - p. 740

(101) *Fermi - The Man & His Theories*, p. deLatil (Translated from French by L. Ortzen)
       Ryerson Press, Toronto 1965 - p. 11

(102) *Experiment With Atomics*, N. Beeler & F. Branley T. Crowell Co., NY
       -1954 - p. 38

(103) *The Second Generation*, R. Crease & C. Mann, MacMillan Co., NY
       -1986 - p. 199

(104) Ibid (93) p. 139

(105) Ibid (93) p. 11

(106) *Niccolo Machiavelli*, Fortune is a woman - H.F. Pitkin. Un. of California Press.
       Berkley 1984 - p. 3

(107) *Machiavelli and Mystery of State*, Peter Donaldson, Cambridge University Press -
       NY 1988

(108) *Encyclopedia Britannica*, 1989 Ed. (The Detailed Study Book)

(109) *The Clock We Live On*, Isaac Asimov, Collier Books - NY. 1963 -pp. 117-142

(110) *World Book Encyclopedia*, Chicago, 1982

(111) *Early European History*, H. Webster, D.C. Heath & Co. Boston 1917 p. 208

(112) Italian Language Course at College of Notre Dame, Baltimore -(Handout Material, Origin Unknown)

(113) *Hanibal, Enemy of Rome*, Leonard Cottrell, 1961

(114) *Letters of Cicero*, L.P. Wilkinson, Hutchinson UN Press, London 1949 (Original Edition) p. 199

APPENDIX

SIMILARITIES IN THE ORGANIZATION OF GOVERNMENT

REPUBLIC OF ROME (founded Approx. 500 B.C.)	REPUBLIC OF THE UNITED STATES (Founded 1789)
<u>CONSTITUTION</u>	<u>CONSTITUTION</u>
Composed of customs, traditions and written laws	A singular written document
<u>EXECUTIVE BRANCH</u> (Administrative Responsibilities)	<u>EXECUTIVE BRANCH</u> (Administrative Responsibilities)
<u>Consuls</u> - Exercised Executive Power	<u>President</u> - Exercises Executive Power
<u>Note:</u> Two consuls were elected to serve concurrently, each having power to veto the acts of the other resulting in a check and balance.	<u>Note:</u> President has veto power over the Legislative branch, resulting in check and balance
<u>Note:</u> Term of office was for one year providing for early termination	<u>Note:</u> Four year term
<u>Junior Consul</u> - (An Assistant - No Power)	<u>Vice President</u> - (Very Little Power)
<u>Administrators</u> - Magistrates and Praetors administered local affairs and justice in the cities.	<u>Cabinet Members</u> - Administrators of sub-departments of government
<u>Procurators</u>- Heads of large provinces	<u>Governors</u> - Heads of individual States

Similarities in the Organization of Government (continued)

REPUBLIC OF ROME (founded Approx. 500 B.C.)	REPUBLIC OF THE UNITED STATES (Founded 1789)
LEGISLATIVE BRANCH	LEGISLATIVE BRANCH
Senate - (Three Hundred)	Senate - (Now one hundred, two from each state)
Duties: Principally to advise and consent and control of foreign affairs. (took extreme pride in its oratorical deliberations)	Duties: Lawmaking, advise and consent and ratification of foreign treaties. (Believed to be the current greatest deliberative body)
Assembly of the People - (Members called Tribunes)	House of Representatives - (Members called Congressmen)
Representatives of the people	Representatives of the people determined by population count
The Assembly proposed the laws to be enacted	Most laws are proposed by the House of Representatives
Veto Power - One individual Tribune could stop the actions of the Senate by calling out "Veto!" (Checks and Balances)	Veto Power - House of Representatives (with Senate) can overcome Presidential veto (checks and Balances).
JUDICIAL BRANCH	JUDICIAL BRANCH
Senatorial Jury Panels - To try high crimes	Supreme Court and System of Federal Courts Power to declare legislated laws and executive orders as being unconstitutional

Similarities in the Organization of Government (continued)

REPUBLIC OF ROME (founded Approx. 500 B.C.)	REPUBLIC OF THE UNITED STATES (Founded 1789)
Censor - An annually selected officer with power to oversee activities of officials and having power to expel a Senator (but not a Tribune, representative of the people a Censor is appointed by the Consul for one year similar to U.S. Attorney General, but with more power and authority)	U.S. Attorney General - Selected by President (the prosecutor of cases involving federal jurisdiction) Senate - Has power to try cases of impeachment
Immunity - Consul and Tribunes were immune from prosecution while in office.	Immunity - President, Senators and Congressmen are granted immunity from prosecution (except treason and felony) and freedom from arrest during attendance or going to or from a session
VOTE	VOTE
Everyone subject to military service (which excluded slaves and women) had the right to vote (1)	Everyone except slaves* and women** were granted the right to vote.
As a citizen, women had all the rights pertaining thereto (property rights, and estate rights, etc.)	* Slavery was abolished and citizenship granted by adoption of the 14th Amendment to the Constitution
Slavery was confined to captured enemies in warfare	** Women were granted the right to vote by adoption of the 19th Amendment in 1920.
Women were granted the right to vote when the modern Republic of Italy was founded and military service excluded in 1946	
(1) *Women in Rome, Law and Society* by Jane Gardner, Indiana University Press (The Library of Notre Dame Preparatory School Towson, MD)	

Similarities in the Organization of Government (continued)

REPUBLIC OF ROME (founded Approx. 500 B.C.)	REPUBLIC OF THE UNITED STATES (Founded 1789)
Other Sources: Constitution of the United States Other references listed in the bibliography and refer also to pages in Book I: 18, 19, 20, 25, 26, 26A	"The art and genius of the Founding Fathers in writing the Constitution of the United States . . . they were wise enough to tap the experience of the ancients." Grollier's Encyclopedia (1966), Book "U", page 146 - United States Government
NOTE Julius Caesar was assassinated for the principal reason that it was believed that he aspired to be king and thus replace the Roman Republic with a monarchy.	The U.S. Constitution provides: Sec. 9, Powers Prohibited To The United States: Absolute Prohibitions On Congress: "No title of nobility shall be granted and no person holding any office. . . shall accept any office or title or any kind whatever from any king, prince, or foreign state.

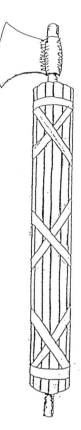

Codexjuris
Symbol of Roman Civil Law on the Doors
of the United States Supreme Court

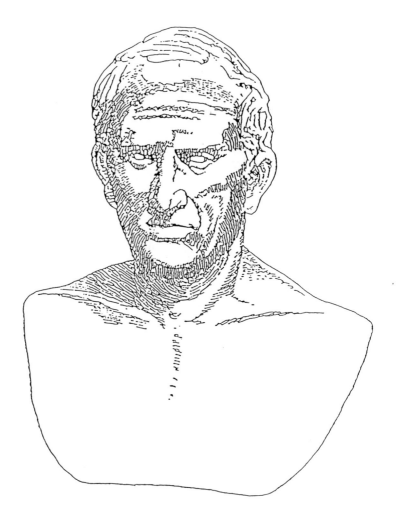

Marcus Tullius Cicero
Vatican Museum, Rome

63

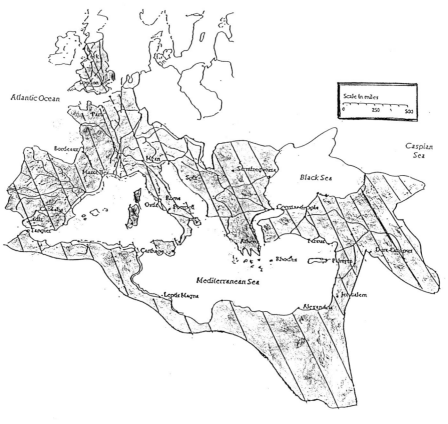

The Roman Empire in 117 A.D.

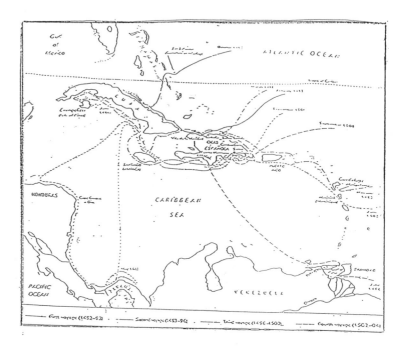

The Voyages of Christopher Columbus

The Maura Medal (Spain), struck to commemorate the Four Hundredth Anniversary of Columbus' Discovery of America

Mosaic portrait of Christopher Columbus by Enrico Podio in Genoa's City Hall

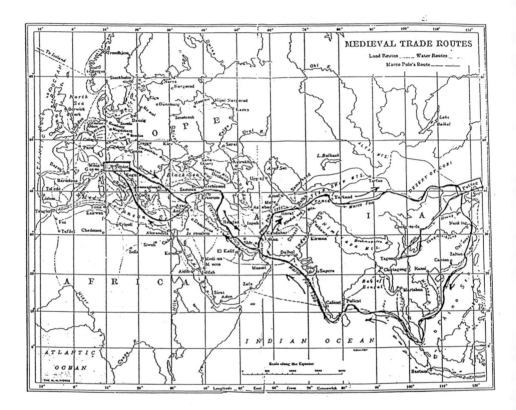

Travels of Marco Polo 1295

Enrico Fermi

Enrico Fermi

FERMI, Enrico (1901-1954), Italian-American physicist, one of the architects of the nuclear age. Fermi won the Nobel Prize in physics in 1938 for his production, by neutron bombardment, of a large number of radioactive isotopes, and for his discovery of the effectiveness of slow neutrons in producing radio activity. His work on nuclear fission, begun in 1939, culminated in the building of the first nuclear reactor and the achievement in it (Dec 2, 1942) of the first sustained nuclear chain reaction. This marked the beginning of the atomic age. This remarkable development of nuclear medicine has been credited as being one of the greatest advancements in health care for diagnosis and treatment of millions of patients annually and extending life expectancy for everyone.

Philip Mazzei (Born Italy - 1730-1819)

PHYSICIAN, MERCHANT, AUTHOR; Ardent supporter of the American Revolution; came to America and wrote extensively in support of American Independence; was a business associate of Thomas Jefferson (wine business) and lived with Jefferson for a while at Monticello (It. "Little Mountain") until his own home and farm were completed next to Jefferson's. Jefferson spoke Italian and was said to have had discourses with Mazzei on principles and theories of government. Mazzei has been credited with urging split branches of governmental responsibility and other principles ultimately finding their way into the U.S. Constitution. He was honored and recognized for his American patriotism by the U.S. Government in 1980 with this postage stamp.

BOOK 2

The Italian Influence
on the
Spread of Christianity

BOOK II INTRODUCTION

Christianity began in a homeless birth and its symbol, a cross, seems to declare its defeat. Yet by 1500 A.D., it had spread more widely than any other religion on earth. "Christianity has become the most potent single force in the life of mankind." (7 p. 7) "Christianity is now deeply rooted in the lives and cultures of approximately one-third of the peoples of the world." (3 p. 5)

The spread of Christianity must be viewed as being influenced by many factors and sources including the early Christians themselves. Other contributing factors were the popes, monastic orders, saints, and the influences outside the Christian community.

Literature on the subject is massive. Fortunately for purposes of research, most of the documentary evidence has been thoroughly examined, translated and reduced to contemporary literature by religious scholars. This virtually unlimited source of material allows for discovery or research into almost any particular question for a reliable answer. References to historical Christianity* will be made where applicable.

In Book II as in Book I, this Treatise is directed to a particular point of view, and that is, the Italian influence on the spread of Christianity. There were, of course, many other non-Italian influences such as the principle one, the Protestant Reformation. As a nation and people, Italians provided a major force and it is on that effort that is focused here.

Also, as in Book I, I trust that this Treatise will provide a good starting point for the student who is interested in further study.

Philip A. Rapisarda 1992

* Christianity is the only religion with historical references.

EARLY HISTORICAL INFLUENCES

It has been said that while Christianity did not originate in Rome, it was Rome that propagated it.

The Roman Emperor Constantine in 313 A.D. issued what has been called the "Edict of Milan" or "Edict of Toleration" (1 p. 57) by which the Roman Empire accorded full legal recognition to Christianity. All previous anti-Christian decrees were revoked, all property restored, and compensation made where possible. This "...was one of the decisive events in world history." (10 p. 67) It proved to be one of the major contributions to its spread. (15 P, 16)

Christianity had its beginnings within the borders of the Roman Empire, and the physical aspects of the Empire were factors in themselves which aided in the spread from one end of the Empire to the other. No other place on earth provided such similarity of culture, language, and feasibility of communication.[3] The central location of Italy in the Mediterranean enabled the freedom of widespread travel with a measure of protection and legality.

The period immediately prior to Emperor Constantine was not a happy one for Christianity. During the era of Pax Romana (a 300 year span of peace, prosperity and generally, political calm and stability), Christianity had undergone several periods of recurrent persecution from many directions.

There was now in place a unified government and system of laws which allowed for a generally accepted principle of freedom of religious practice. During this period, Christianity ran headlong into a problem. It was during this time that the cult of emperor-worship arose, and the emperors demanded to be worshiped as gods. However, not all of the emperors enforced this cult with the same determination. The worst offenders were Domitian, Hadrian and Diocletian. (Diocletian took the title "Master and God.") The Jews were the only religious group exempted from the requirement of emperor worship. (2 p. 71) Christians were strongly against this practice and those who refused were violently punished or put to death. This period of persecution is mentioned, not for purposes of histrionics, but because it ushers in certain influences of a personal nature affecting the spread of Christianity such as the

---

[3] See Roman Road system map

influence resulting from martyrdom. Oddly enough "Christians were accused of atheism for not worshiping the 'emperor as a god'." "Christians were required to sacrifice to the pagan gods, offer prayer and libations of wine to images of the emperor, and speak ill of Christ." (12 p. 60) Refusal was a capital offense punishable by death. (12 pp. 52 and 59)

The early Christians took a beating, literally, from government and private sources. For instance, Constantine's Edict (in 313 A.D.) outlawed the practice of stoning to death others who converted to Christianity, and persecution was not all in the "Arena" as it is commonly depicted. The first such recorded martyr was St. Stephen. It is said that St. Paul (during the period of his life when he was persecuting the Christians) was present at the stoning of St. Stephen and may have actually participated. This was, of course, prior to his miraculous conversion. He was unable to erase from his memory the radiant face of St. Stephen as he prayed to God to forgive his tormentors. This event is often referred to as an example of how martyrdom affected others. The lifestyle and personal courage demonstrated by Christians being persecuted and martyred had profound effect. These thousands of victims are to be counted as those who unknowingly aided in the spread of Christianity. Tertullian wrote (in 196 A.D.) "The blood of martyrs is seed." Most of these nameless souls were Italians because, unfortunately, the closer one was to the source of power, Rome, the more strictly enforced was the cult of emperor worship. Christianity is believed to have more martyrs than any other religion. (3 p. 81) The steadfastness of the Christians in the face of death evoked widespread sympathy and wonder. "Countless Christians perished, including Pope Marcellinus, in 304 A.D." (15 p. 16)

Many Roman soldiers were converted to Christianity by the example of the victims of persecution and many were later recognized for their Christian works after conversion and later canonized (refer to the list of Saints). The Roman soldiers that marched from one end of the Empire to the other aided in the spreading of Christianity. "Rome was the instrument whereby Christianity first reached Western Europe...was almost certainly introduced by soldiers who had seen service in the East." (1 p. 22)

Two such saints, St. Nereus and St. Achilleus (celebrated in the Roman Catholic calendar on May 12th), were Roman soldiers who were both martyred for their faith. They are buried in the cemetery of Domnitilla on Via Ardeatina outside Rome, and the statue of Achilleus is the earliest known representation of a martyr. He was martyred in the First Century. (9 p. 188)

The good news of the Gospels was spread at every opportunity, and it became impossible to prevent nomatter how aggressive the effort. The following is a copy of the famous *Letter to Diognetus* written about the second century. It clearly describes the extraordinary characteristics of the Christians.

THE LETTER TO DIOGNETUS (Somewhere in the Middle East)

"For Christians are not differentiated from other people by country, language or customs; you see, they do not live in cities of their own, or speak some strange dialect, or have some peculiar lifestyle.

This teaching of theirs has not been contrived by the invention and speculation of inquisitive men; nor are they propagating mere human teaching as some people do. They live in both Greek and foreign cities, wherever chance has put them. They follow local customs in clothing, food and the other aspects of life. But at the same time, they demonstrate to us the wonderful and certainly unusual form of their own citizenship.

They live in their own native lands, but as aliens, as citizens, they share all things with others; but like aliens, suffer all things. Every foreign country is to them as their native country and every native land as a foreign country.

They marry and have children just like everyone else, but they do not kill unwanted babies. They offer a shared table, but not a bed. They are at present "in the flesh" but they do not live "according to the flesh." They are passing their days on earth, but are citizens of heaven. They obey the appointed laws and go beyond the laws in their own lives.

They love everyone but are persecuted by all. They are unknown and condemned; they are put to death and gain life. They are poor and yet make many rich. They are short of everything and yet have plenty of all things. They are dishonored and yet gain glory through dishonor.

Their names are blackened and yet they are cleared. They are mocked and bless in return. They are treated outrageously and behave respectfully to others. When they do good, they are punished as evildoers; when punished, they rejoice as if being given new life. They are attacked by Jews as aliens and are persecuted by Greeks; yet those who hate them cannot give any reason for their hostility.

To put it simply--the soul is to the body as Christians are in the world. The soul is spread through all parts of the body and Christians through all the cities of the world. The soul is in the body but is not of the world. The soul is in the body, but is not of the body; Christians are in the world, but not of the world."

The letter illustrates an increased awareness of the spiritual nature of Christianity. Christianity erased the distinctions between the classes, high or low, free or slave, and in an era where strange cults, multiple gods and pagan practices were prevalent, Christianity displayed stark contrast. This new lifestyle against a backdrop of the Old Testament teaching of vengeance and an "eye for an eye", the Christian message of humility, love and turning the other cheek was literally "out of this world." By his personal example, each Christian was both a priest and a missionary.

In the first 500 years, Christianity made such overwhelming strides in the conversion of peoples of all nationalities that it was said that Christianity conquered the Roman Empire itself. (3 p. 65) The proselytizing was so intense (even against many competing religious sects and cults) that it reached to the highest levels of authority, to the Emperor and his family.

We know through St. Paul's letters to the Romans that there was a large Christian community in Rome. Keep in mind that his letters were written within approximately fifty years of the crucifixion of Jesus. The citizens of Rome were active in the dramatic spread of the Faith and Christianity throughout the Empire. Christianity then began to spread beyond the borders of the Empire and there were approximately one hundred Bishoprics in Italy, as opposed to about twenty in all of Asia Minor (3 pp. 77-79) "The Church of Rome occupied an outstanding place in the total Christian fellowship." (3 P 118)

<u>The Edict of Milan</u> 313 A.D.(The world's first law granting Christians the Freedom to practice their religion)

To better understand the great change and impetus generated by Emperor Constantine by the Edict of Milan, a brief review of its principle provisions are as follows:

1. An immediate cessation of persecution of Christians.
2. Freed the Christian clergy from contributions to the State.
3. Allowed wills in favor of the Church.
4. Sunday was accorded the same legal status as pagan feasts.
5. Provincial governors were instructed to honor the memory of Christian martyrs and Christian festivals.
6. Forbade members of current Orthodox Religious groups from stoning their co-religionists who chose to become Christians.
7. Built and enlarged churches.
8. Prohibited forcing Christians to practice non-Christian rituals or practices.
9. Prohibited the repair of pagan temples.
10. Emperor Constantine took an active part in Church Affairs.
11. He called for and presided over the first general council of the Church.
12. Emperor Constantine accepted baptism of himself.
    (All of the above in 3 p. 93)

13. Outlawed crucifixion.
14. Forbade face branding of slaves and criminals as all men were made in the image of God.
15. Made the Imperial Privy liable for upkeep of poor children.
16. Outlawed gladiatorial combat.
17. Made Sunday a public holiday.
    (13 to 17 can be found in 7 pp. 23-24)

The sons of Constantine were also positive toward Christianity. In 341 A.D., his second son not only ordered all pagan practices abolished, but also closed all pagan temples. These edicts were effective throughout the Empire and the result was that Christians became the overwhelming majority of the population of the Roman Empire. (3 p. 221)

By now many Christians from every province of the Empire and beyond were vigorously at work preaching the Gospels, converting the pagans and establishing churches everywhere.

Christianity was now firmly established, but not without problems, substantial pressures from outside cults, and from heretics within.

The histrionics of Christianity are not intended here, but a brief mention of some events must be made (such as the decline after 500 A.D.) because Italians played a significant role in its reformation.

The Roman Empire continued to disintegrate and the invasions by the Moslems of the East and South and the barbarians of the North also had a decided and weakening effect upon Christianity as well. Therefore, substituting for the government, the Christian Church and its organization took on many of the functions necessary for civil community living. Christianity then became the principal protector of the weak, the poor, the widows and orphans, and provided the elements of justice and stability.

The circumstances of the world's instability required that the Pope step in and act as a secular ruler in the face of a vacant civil authority.

However, political rule was not the Pope's specialty. The Church itself became divided, as was the government, and it became prey to power hungry ecclesiastics who were being manipulated by the nobility. Many of the evils and errors that had crept into the Church were traceable to the corrupt hierarchy. Christianity persisted and continued to spread, but not with the same vigorous growth of the first 500 years.

Although this was a sad period (and commentary) on the Christian ecclesiastics, nevertheless, they passed on a highly significant bequest. This was the preservation, through the Church and its monasteries, of much of the civilization of the Roman Empire and its transmission to later generations. (3 p. 370)

MONASTERIES AND ORDERS:

The monasteries became the centers of stability, learning, and piety. The spread of Christianity through the establishment of religious orders and congregations proceeded at a steady pace for many centuries, and Italians were the most active founders of religious orders, congregations, and missions.

An early figure in the emergence of the monastic movement was Cassidorious. He founded two monasteries, one for ascetic life and one for learning; he pioneered the idea of a scriptorium (a room in the monastery used for writing) and a refined and quiet area for study. He supervised the translation from Greek to Latin the works of important Christians and historians, and his writings formed the basic educational curriculum of the period.

The following (not in any particular order) are the more prominent monasteries:

One of the most vigorous and influential figures in the monastic movement was St. Benedict of Nursia(480-547), the founder of the great Benedictine Monastic System and what became known as the Benedictine Rule. These were rules of organization, purpose and rules for perpetuation. The "Rule of Benedict" (2 p. 213) became the most copied, as well as the format, for most future monasteries. It spread throughout all of Western Europe and was generally accepted everywhere.

The spreading monastic system became the more successful method of carrying the message of the Gospels, and Benedictine monks became very prominent as missionaries.

Pope Gregory I The Great sent a group of missionaries headed by a monk named Augustine (not Augustine of Hippo) to England in about 600 A.D., and he became the first Archbishop of Canterbury. The missionaries were from a monastery which had been founded by Pope Gregory I. "Within a century after the arrival of Augustine, missionaries from the recently converted English were going back to the continent... They lead in the conversion of much of what is now Holland and Germany, organized the Church there and tied it with Rome." (3 pp. 345-347)

The power and authority of the Pope was added to the monastic movement. Pope Gregory I (a.k.a. Gregory The Great), of a wealthy family, founded and endowed six monasteries as well as supporting the development of others. He turned his ancestral home in Rome into a monastery and the remainder of his inheritance was given to the poor. Much of the authentic documentation and information concerning Benedict was recorded and preserved by Pope Gregory I. The Benedictine Rule is still followed today.

The following (not in any particular order) are other monastic orders inspired, founded or substantially assisted by Italians:

Franciscan - Order of Little Brothers, Friars Minor (Ordo Fratrum Minoum) O.F.M. Founded by Francis of Assisi (1181-1226), baptismal name Giovanni. It has become the largest order and flourished under the "Rule of Francis." He also founded a second order through St. Clare of Assisi for cloistered nuns and a third order for religious and laity of both sexes.

Augustinians - Groups of clergymen recognized the need to work among the population rather than in a cloistered community and used the Augustinian Rule, where possible, in their mission among the people. This was a less costly method of monastic life and it became very popular, especially as the cities grew in size. (3 p. 400)

Servites - (Servants of Mary) Founded by seven Florentine youths in 1304. Bongiglio Monaldo, Bonaiunta Manetto, Manetto Antellese, Amadeo Amedie, Uguccione Uguccioni, Sosteno Sostenei and Allessio Falconieri.

Sylvestrines - Founded by Sylvester Gozzolini. Followed the "Rule of Benedict." This order, although not as numerous, has survived to the Twentieth Century.

Olivetans - Founded by a small group of aristocrats from Sienna, in 1313. They followed the "Rule of Benedict."

Carthusian - This order was not founded by an Italian, but is included here because its fifth Prior, Bruno, is credited with giving the new and small order the impulse to develop and expand as it founded additional houses and attracted many followers.

Redemptorist - (Congregation of the Most Holy Redeemer) Founded by Alpitonsus Maria Liguori in 1732. They specialized in preaching the dire consequences of sin and made themselves available for retreats and Lenten missions.

Jesuati - Founded by John Colombini (1300-1367) of Sienna. They gave themselves to the care of the sick, especially those stricken by the plague and to the burial of the dead.

Oblates - Founded by St. Frances of Rome (1384-1440). Followed the "Benedictine Rule" and gave themselves to prayer and good works. (3 p. 654)

Minims - A strict order of Franciscan monks founded by Francis of Paola, Calabria in 1517. Dedicated to prayer and study. (3 p. 658)

<u>Order of the Regular Clerics Minor</u> Founded by St. Francis Caracciolo of Naples (1550-1608). He was one of the three founders of the order serving those in prison. (The other two members were Augustine Adorno and Fabricius Caracciolo.) His original name was Ascanio Caracciolo, but he changed it to Francis in honor of Francis of Assisi.

<u>Order of Poor Clares</u> Founded by St. Clare of Assisi (1193-1253) and devoted to work among the poor.

<u>Order of Camadulian</u> Named after the center of Camadoli, Italy where the Mother house is located. It was founded by St. Romauld of Ravenna and was dedicated to prayer, preaching and good works.

<u>Order of Clerics Regular of St. Paul</u> Founded by St. Anthony Zaccaria (1502-1539) of Cremona and was dedicated to preaching and frequent administration of the Sacraments. He also founded the Community of Angelicals with the aim of rescuing separated Christians.

<u>Order of Vallombrosa</u> Founded by St. John Gualbert (993-1073) who was born near Camaldoli and he also founded the monastery of Vallombrusa near Florence. Dedicated to prayer and perpetual silence.

<u>Order of Clerics Regular for the Sick</u> Founded by St. Camillus (1550-1614), born near Naples. The Order was devoted to caring for the sick and dying.

<u>Congregation of the Most Holy Redeemer</u> Founded by St. Alphonsus Liguori (1696-1787) born near Marinella, Naples. The Order was devoted to laboring for the salvation of the most abandoned souls.

<u>Order of Clerics Regular of Mother of God</u> Founded by St. John Leonardi (1541-1609). Born in Decimi near Lucca. The Order was devoted to conversion of sinners and return of discipline to the Church. He was also co-founder (with Cardinal Vives) of the College of Propaganda and Preaching for the propagation of the Faith.

<u>Missionary Sisters of the Sacred Heart</u> Founded by St. Frances Xavier Cabrini (1850-1917), born in Lombardy, Italy. The Order was dedicated to the care of poor children in schools and hospitals. She came to America, became a citizen and worked among Italian immigrants. She later founded houses in England, France, Spain, and South America. Mother Cabrini became the first American citizen to be canonized.

<u>Pallotines</u> - (Pique Society of Missions) Founded by Vincent Mary Pallotti (1789-1858), born in Rome. Devoted to the physical and spiritual care of the poor and sick. Its members included laymen, priests and sisters.

<u>Salesians of Don Bosco</u> - (1815-1888) Devoted to missionary work among underprivileged children.

<u>Congregation of the Most Precious Blood</u> Founded by Gaspare del Bufalo (1786-1837), born in Rome. Devoted to instruction, works of charity and propagating devotion to the Most Precious Blood.

<u>Order of the Visitation</u> Founded by both Francis deSales and St. Jane deChantal. The Order was devoted to teaching and preaching the importance of piety of the laity.

<u>Order of Celestines</u> Founded by St. Peter Celestine and was devoted to teaching, counseling, good works and prayer.

<u>Order of Ursulines</u> Founded by St. Angela Merici. This was the first teaching order of the Church.

<u>Congregation of Williamites</u> Founded by St. William and was dedicated to helping the poor and prayering to the Blessed Virgin.

<u>Order of Clevics Regular of Somascha</u> Founded by St. Jerome Emilliani. The order was dedicated to the care of orphans and the sick.

MISSIONS

All nationalities were participants in the missionary movements throughout the world, but the overwhelming majority of new movements and permanent monasteries had their origin in Italy. In some movements and orders founded by non-Italians "the leaders who later did most to give the foundation widespread distinction were from Italy." (3 p. 343) At one time, it was estimated that there were approximately 100,000 Franciscans.

The first Christian missionary to reach China was a Franciscan Monk named John of Montecorvino. In 1294 he bore a letter from the Pope to Khubilai Khan. (Note: This was one year before the return of Marco Polo (1295) to Venice from his travels to the Orient.) John established a church there in 1305, had 6,000 converts and translated the New Testament and Psalter into the local language. (3 p. 403) As a result of his success, the Pope sent seven more Franciscans and consecrated them Bishops with authority to consecrate. John was made the first Archbishop of China.

A missionary of the Theatine Order from Palermo was called the "Apostle of Borneo" and became the first Vicar Apostolic on that Island. (7 Vol II p. 935)

The leading missionary to Macao was Matteo Ricci (1552-1610). He was a diligent student of Chinese and adapted the Gospels to Chinese tradition, thought, and form. (7 Vol. II p. 939)

Robert Di Noboli (1577-1656) served in India and adapted the Gospels to the local Indian culture.

Perhaps the most recognized missionary was St. Patrick (389 ? -461). His Italian name was Palladius, son of Calpurnius and Conchessa. He was commissioned by Pope Leo the Great to organize the Church in Ireland and history has recorded his remarkable success.

Part of the success of the mission movement was due to the wise instruction given to the missionaries. "Do not regard it as your task, and do not bring any pressure to bear on the peoples to change their manners, customs, and uses, unless they are evidently contrary to religion and sound morals... Introduce them to only the faith which does not effect the manners and customs of any people." (2 p. 465) Most of the missionaries were zealous workers and it was chiefly through them that Christianity spread throughout the world.

Many of the orders and missions performed multiple functions, but most were devoted to prayer, charity and missionary works. One important function carried on in the monasteries was the recording and preservation of historical events and documents.

The importance of this function cannot be emphasized enough, as Christianity is the only historical and documented religion. Jesus' earthly mission is recorded by the historians Josephus, Tacitus, Pliny the Younger, and Suetonius, as well as the letters of St. Paul. (10 pp. 23-24) These documents have been preserved, recorded and handed down to subsequent generations of monastery monks. "There exists today about 4,700 manuscripts and about 100,000 quotations or allusions to the early fathers." (10 p. 26) The importance of this wealth of documentation becomes vital because of the need for clarification and theological interpretations.

THE INFLUENCE OF THEOLOGY

A brief definition could be the study of the relationship between God and man.

In the very early days of Christianity there was no organized method of training priests, nor was there what could be described as an institutional church. Learning consisted principally of reading the scriptures and overseeing the functions needed for the administration of one's duties. It was a form of apprenticeship.

The need for theology was apparent to advance the teaching of Christianity so as to provide an understanding of God, rather than a mere belief in God. This would be necessary to provide a strengthening of the faith and for resistance against the relentless opposition by heretics, pagans, cults, and other religions. Theology provided a kind of wall of defense, as well as the element of progress, and it later became a science and an organized body of knowledge.

The thoughts and writings of the theologians became a necessary and vital element in the passage of Christianity through the centuries. The philosophical questions and the rationality of their relationship to God were constantly being questioned and answers were needed.

One of the very earliest thinkers in the style of a theologian was Tertullian. He was born in Carthage, North Africa of Italian parentage about 150 A.D. Carthage was the North African Capital of the Roman Empire. (3 p. 77)

Tertullian was the first major author to write in Latin. He also translated many works from Greek to Latin and, amazingly, 31 of his Latin books have survived to this day. He was the first to develop the doctrine of the "Trinity" as "One God" and he is often referred to as the Father of Latin Theology.

It was not until the coming of St. Augustine of Hippo in the last decades of the Fourth Century that theology began to establish itself as a separate scientific field of inquiry. Keeping within the limits of our subject, Italian influences, the following are a few of the more notable theologians who were either Italian or early in life "Italianized." They are not listed in any rigid order.

Theologians

St. Augustine of Hippo - (354-430) It is believed he was of Italian stock. (3 p. 96) His ancestors had emigrated from Italy to North Africa. (3 p. 77) His birth name was Aurelius Augustinus (16 p. 700) and his mother, Monica, was also canonized. St. Augustine was a prolific author and his writings became Christian classics; and his works, on the rule of religious life, were a great influence in the spiritual life of Western Christianity. His book, the *Confessions of Augustine*, is still available in bookstores and is one of the important documents of Christian faith. (7 p. 851) He was made Bishop and Doctor of the Church and is considered one of the earliest of the classic theologians. He gives great credit to the writings and philosophy of Cicero, (a pre-Christian), in forming his conversion to Christianity. (Refer to section on "Cicero" in Book I.)

St. Ambrose of Milan - (339-397) He was born of a noble Roman family in North Italy (where his father had been appointed Prefect) and they returned to Rome in his infancy. He too was a prolific writer and his works are of considerable influence in theology. It was Ambrose, as Bishop of Milan, who converted and baptized Augustine of Hippo in 387 A.D. He was the first to introduce community singing in church, and he was also awarded the title of Doctor of the Church.

Pope Gregory I The Great - (540-604) He is also known as St. Gregory. The son of Roman Senator Gordianus, was the first to be elevated to the Papacy (who had previously been a monk), and was recognized as one of the strongest Popes in history.

"More than any other man, Gregory laid the foundation for the power which the Church of Rome was to exercise in Western Europe." (3 Vol. I p. 339) He proclaimed the supreme authority of the Papacy over all Christendom. "Gregory was not only an administrator, but in later centuries he was more famous as a theologian...and did much to fix its beliefs." (3 pp. 340-341) Of long term importance was his sending of a team of monks from the monastery he founded to Christianize Britain. The effort was an outstanding success. As a result he was awarded the title of Doctor of the Church, and is one of only two Popes accorded the honor of being called "The Great." (Pope Leo I was the other.) His writings included books used in the training of clergy, and he also encouraged music in the celebration of the Mass. (The Gregorian Chant is still in use today.)

St. Anselm - (1033-1109) was born in Piedmont, Italy of noble parentage. He was a profound thinker, a prodigious writer, and was known as the Father of Scholasticism. Anselm is honored as a philosopher and theologian and was the first to develop the idea that the existence of God could be proved by reason. "God is that which no greater can be conceived." His greatest work was his thesis, *Why Did God Become Man?* "Mankind gains salvation through the merits of Christ." Anselm was also instrumental in suppressing slave trade and advancing the principle of human freedom. He later became Archbishop of Canterbury and was honored as a Doctor of the Church.

St. Thomas Aquinas (1225-1274) was born in Aquino, Italy. He was the most outstanding theologian of the Middle Ages and perhaps in the entire history of the Catholic Church. His writings filled 20 large volumes and provided an encyclopedia source of Christian thought. "Thomas' work gained prominence in Roman Catholic thought which it has retained to the present time." (3 Vol. I p. 238) "What the Roman Catholic Church of the Twentieth Century adjudged the Standard Formulation of Theology was by Thomas Aquinas." (3 Vol.I p. 495) It is looked to as providing the systematic intellectual statement of Roman Catholic Faith. His work is considered the high point of scholasticism and he is known as the Prince of School Men. Aquinas, as Anselm, attempted to show that faith and reason are not inconsistent. After the collapse of the Roman Empire and the resulting decline of Christianity, the struggle for

Catholic Reformation received his crucial support at the Council of Trent (1545-1563). "The Roman Catholic reformers used the works of Aquinas in drafting their decrees and in 1879 Pope Leo XIII declared "Thomasism," Aquinas' theology, eternally valid." (3 Vol. I p. 388) He is a Doctor of the Church and was the first to receive the degree.

Robert Bellarmine (1542-1621) was born in Tuscany. He was the nephew of Pope Paul III and an early Jesuit. While not considered a theologian in the classic sense, he actively participated in the defense of the Catholic Faith. "He wrote what was probably the ablest defense of the Roman Catholic Faith from the attacks of Protestantism during the Sixteenth Century." (7 Vol. II p. 849)

Theology and theologians, as an influence in the spread of Christianity, is typified in the very early example of St. Justin Martyr (100- ?-165). He was not of Italian ancestry. Justin was not the theologian as is characterized previously herein. However, his extensive writings are of special importance to Christianity. His works are invaluable as they contained reliable documentation on Christian Faith and practice at that time. (9 p. 220) Two of his most important works are:

1. *Apologies* (meaning defense and explanations), Letters to Emperor Antonius setting forth the moral values of Christianity.
2. *Dialogue*, Writings to demonstrate the truths of Christianity to the Jewish historian, Trypho.

He was later denounced and martyred with six of his adherents in about 165 A.D. His writings were an inspiration, which aided in their being preserved, and are still in existence to this day. He is considered an example of how theology influenced the spread and establishment of the Christian Faith. (He is included here to stress the importance of theology.)

Teachers and writers made theology a major subject in the early universities. An example is the University of Bologna, Italy, one of the first and earliest universities established in the Western World.

Prominent among many great scholars of the early universities was John of Fidanza (1221-1274) better known as Bonaventura, a head of the Franciscans, and called the Doctor of Seraphicus. He was later appointed Bishop of Albano and a Cardinal. His writings on theology gained wide respect.

<u>St. Jerome of Stridonium</u> (345-420) Was born near Venice and regarded as perhaps the greatest Biblical Scholar in all of Christendom. His writings were extensive and applied to many aspects of Christian beliefs and personal relationships. The conceptions he expressed often stirred great controversy, especially in matters concerning sex, marriage and celibacy in the priesthood. These controversies have persisted to the Twentieth Century and many of his books still exist to this day, having been preserved in monasteries and in the Vatican Library. The style of writing and expressions used were often sharp and incisive, leaving little room for alternate positions.

He is also recognized for his brilliant Biblical study and his monumental translation of the Old and New Testaments. The translation was from Greek and Hebrew into Latin and is known as the Vulgate Bible. This unprecedented scriptural accomplishment took twenty-three years to complete and required him to become fluent in Greek and Hebrew.

St. Jerome is regarded as one of the five greatest "Doctors of the Church." The other four in this category are: St. Augustine of Hippo, St. Ambrose of Milan, St. Gregory the Great and St. Thomas Aquinas. (See previous specific details on each.)

"DOCTOR OF THE CHURCH" - The distinction of the title carries with it honor, respectability, and recognition for extraordinary accomplishments. Very few have been so honored and accorded the title. Of the approximately three hundred Popes and thousands of religious of every level of clerical vocation, only about thirty-five have been so honored in two thousand years. Of that number, almost half, seventeen, were of Italian Heritage. The following is a list of the seventeen:

St. Augustine of Hippo	- Bishop, Doctor, Theologian
St. Ambrose of Milan	- Bishop, Doctor, Theologian
St. Gregory I (Great)	- Pope, Doctor, Theologian
St. Jerome of Stridonium	- Doctor, Biblical Scholar
St. Leo I (Great)	- Pope, Doctor
St. Alphonsus	- Bishop, Doctor
St. Thomas Aquinas	- Priest, Doctor, Theologian
St. Anselm	- Bishop, Doctor, Theologian
St. Catherine of Sienna	- Religious, Doctor
St. Bonaventure	- Bishop, Doctor
St. Lawrence Brindisi	- Priest, Doctor
St. Peter Chrysologus	- Bishop, Doctor
St. Robert Bellarmine	- Bishop, Doctor, Theologian
St. Peter Damian	- Bishop, Doctor
St. Benedict of Nursia	- Abbot, Doctor
St. Francis deSales	- Bishop, Doctor
St. Anthony of Padua	- Priest, Doctor

PREFACE TO POPES

The Pope is probably the most unique "head of state" in the world. No other national leader has the standing to create an "event" by his mere presence or by his issuance of a declaration or communication. He is also perhaps the most respected "head of state", secular or religious, and is accorded this dignity in every manner of contact, whatever the level of importance or status of the parties.

It is now about two thousand years and three hundred Popes since the advent of Christianity. In the course of this period, momentous events have occurred, severe periods of economic and political dislocations, and attempts by one power or another to gain domination over another nation or authority including the Papacy. The Papacy was often the target of these struggles causing it to take whatever means available for survival. During these dark periods, of which there were many, there was no such thing as "rights" except to those that had the "might" to assert them. As a result, in some periods, some Popes were merely the products of their times. There were some outstanding ones who resisted, and some not so outstanding, very similar to their secular counterparts.

In the secular world, families fought against each other in struggles for power and struggles occurred in Christianity, where tradition resisted heresy and schism.

The early Popes, and those after the Catholic Reformation, maintained a high standard of morality, intelligence and ability; they inspired leadership, performance of duty, and responsibility.

During the Middle Ages, certain Popes fell under the power of emperors and nobles, but were few and they were the exception. Historians charge Pope Alexander VI (1492-1503) of the Spanish Borgia family with having the poorest record of administration. (13 p. 161)

This treatise is concerned with, and is sympathetic to, the beneficial influence of Italians on the spread of Christianity and not on any individual's shortcomings during the two thousand year period when Italians were often central to the cause. Therefore where there was depression, they were a part of it. But conversely, their beneficial influence was of major proportion.

Of the approximately three hundred Popes, only two were accorded the added honor and title "The Great": Pope Leo I and Pope Gregory I, both of Italian heritage.

ITALIAN POPES
Partial List and Noteworthy Events of Their Reign

Pope Julius I (337-352) was born in Rome and later became Bishop of Rome. After becoming Pope, he was very early thrust into a sharp controversy and near schism concerning Arian heresy.

His manner was forceful and direct. He was not afraid to assert himself against anyone, regardless of their exalted position. As a result of his firm belief in the correctness of his position, his influence became widespread and "for the first time, the Pope emerged as an international figure with prestige in the Roman World greatly enhanced." (8 p. 20)

Pope Innocent I (402-417) was believed to have been born near Rome. Upon ascending the Papacy he pursued with vision the independence and superiority of the Roman Papacy in Christian affairs throughout the world. It was he who established the principle that any spiritual declaration or action initiated in the provinces could not take effect without his approval.

His personality and strong will was such that he met face to face with Alaric and his invading Goths on the outskirts of Rome. Alaric was persuaded to concede that while he would plunder Rome, the population should not be harmed, and after three days, his Goths left the city. Historians have also accorded him special recognition for his ability and influence in resolving several serious heretical controversies.

Pope Leo I The Great (440-451) His family name is not certain, but he was born in Tuscany, Italy and was the first Pope to be given the added title "The Great." (The only other was Pope Gregory I) The accolades concerning him are many. "He towers like a second rock of St. Peter in the midst of a century fraught with dread and disaster" . . He turned out to be the perfect Pope in an era of uncertainty." (8 p. 26)

He secured a decree confirming Rome's absolute primacy of the Apostolic See. This momentous and important decree declared that the Popes automatically received and conferred, to all successors, the authority directly from Christ to Peter and on down. Pope Leo also established the doctrine of infallibility of the Pope in matters of doctrine. Over fifteen of his letters still survive.

Pope Leo (as Pope Innocent I did fifty years prior with Alaric) met with Atilla

"The Hun" in 450 A.D. and also dissuaded him from destroying Rome and avoiding loss of life, a very remarkable duplication. He was awarded the honor and title of Doctor of the Church.

<u>Pope Gregory I The Great</u> (590-604). He was born into a wealthy Roman family that produced two prior Popes, Felix III (his great grandfather) and Agapetus I. His family name was Gordianus. (For more details on Pope Gregory I The Great, refer to the sections on Monasteries and Orders and on Theology.)

<u>Pope Gregory II</u> (715-731) was a native Roman. He was a distinguished administrator and diplomat and made a great contribution to stabilization and guidance of Christianity through a very chaotic period.

By now Rome had become a mere ghost of its former self. What remained of the Roman Empire was now directed from Constantinople by Emperor Leo who was thrashing Italy for more taxes to pay for his wars in Asia. At the same time, King Liutprand of Lombardy marched into Italy from the north and held the city at his mercy. Pope Gregory II met King Liutprand at the approaches to Rome and as Pope Innocent I and Pope Leo I did hundreds of years prior, persuaded him not to harm the population nor destroy the undefended city of Rome.

His religious position was that no power could hope to control Italy unless it was with the permission of the Church. This stunning and audacious position of Papal supremacy was an outstanding triumph, as it came at a crucial time: when Islam was sweeping Christianity from North Africa, Spain, and threatening to eclipse Christianity as a major religion.

<u>Pope Stephen II</u> (752-757) was born in Rome. Through his exceptional diplomacy and the great respect that was accorded him, he was also able to save Rome and its people from a blood-bath and destruction by King Alstulf of the Lombards in 755. In his religious life, he was an example of piety, courage, intelligence, and was credited with raising the prestige of Papal authority. This was the fourth time that Rome and its people were saved from devastation by the intervention of a Pope.

Pope Hadrain I (772-795) was of Roman stock and was among the ablest of pontiffs. He performed with diligence and success in overcoming many delicate matters both religious and secular.

He is also credited with restoring much of the City of Rome to its former splendor, clearing most of what had been devastated by the many invasions. New churches were built and old ones restored, refurbished and redecorated with elaborate mosaics.

Nicholas I (858-867) He was of Roman birth, instilled with high ideals, and a strong belief of his spiritual mission as Christ's representative on earth and true guardian of the faith. He had unwavering faith in defending the church's sphere of influence and never backed away from a fight. He stood fast and denied an annulment to Frankish King Lothar II who intended to marry his mistress. He denied this in the face of King Lothar's menacing soldiers at the gates of Rome, and thus strengthened the status and independence of the Papal office and supremacy of the Roman Church. "Nicholas I raised Papal prestige to an unprecedented height." (8 p. 71)

Pope Gregory VII Hildebrand (1073-1085) was the son of a poor Tuscan carpenter and was raised in Rome. As an administrator and as chief policy maker, he was the power behind the throne of the prior Pope, Honorious II. He is said to have been steadfast of character and devoted to principle. His prime contribution was a decree of substantial significance toward independence and supremacy of the Papacy. He prohibited the investure of any cleric who was a layman no matter how exalted that layman may be, even if he was the King.

It was expected that he would not be so bold as to attempt to enforce it, but he was firm. Furthermore, in his "Dictas Papas", he laid down additional Papal decrees to strengthen the Papacy. Some of the more bold and prominent ones were:
1.   The Roman church had never erred and would never err.
2.   The Pope had the sole right to be called "Universal."
3.   The Pope is the sole judge of all matters spiritual and secular.
4.   In the Christian world, in "major causes", he cannot be judged by anyone on earth.
5.   He had the power to depose emperors and kings and their servants.

6. He alone could depose bishops.
7. No decree of a Synod is valid without his approval.
8. The Pope had the power to release subjects from allegiance to their King.
9. No King or Emperor could, on his own, appoint a cleric.

This ideology appeared to finalize 1000 years of ascending Papal independence and supremacy.

An amazing sequence of events then took place. King Henry IV appointed the Bishop of Milan. The Pope very vigorously demanded it to be retracted. King Henry responded by demanding the removal of the Pope. The Pope countered by declaring that King Henry was no longer King, all his subjects were released of their allegiance to him and that furthermore, he was henceforth excommunicated.

This bewildering situation was gradually brought to a close over the next several years by a cooling off period. Neither side capitulated. King Henry's troops gradually withdrew to a monastery at Monte Casino. Pope Gregory VI was accorded great respect and honor as probably the most outstanding Pope since Gregory I The Great.

This dispute simmered on however, sometimes hot and sometimes cool. The next Pope, Urban II, attempted to resolve the matter in favor of the Papacy. It boiled over again 30 years later, won by the sovereign, only to be rewon again by the Church 10 years later.

This scenario continued for another 100 years with the "lead" shifting from one side to the other. Eventually the emperors' side prevailed, more or less, military "might" was "right." Despite this standoff, the Papacy pressed on until Pope Alexander III (July 28, 1177), at which time the Emperor capitulated. Still the matter did not end, because future emperors came on the scene with their own ideas. The "see-saw" was back again, but with less vigor, and in 1346 (300 years after it began) the Papacy appeared to prevail but it continued to smolder for many more years.

Pope Alexander III (1159-1181). His family name was Bandinetti (of Siena). He was another very strong-willed Pope who strengthened the supremacy of the Papal Office. (Refer above to text on Pope Gregory VI) He regained all lands and revenues that had been wrongfully taken away during the previous 75 years. He was described as an experienced statesman and diplomat of steady temperament, and was capable of satisfactorily standing up to the confrontation of experienced lawyers from Bologna.

He was said to have had remarkable stamina. "It is impossible not to admire Alexander's achievements in withstanding for so many years, and finally frustrating, the aims of the mightiest ruler of that age." (8 p. 121)

"His tactics were perfectly effective,...he never lost his head or his nerve, ... tenacious and resilient are epithets historians have applied to his character...above all he was a superb administrator." (8 p. 121) "The Papacy emerged from the long conflict with dignity and greatly enhanced." (15 p. 121) He was also an eminent jurist handling an enormous volume of transactions which inspired a vast output of decrees contributing to Canon Law.

Pope Innocent III (1198-1216), the son of a noble Roman family, was trained in theology and law. He was a tower of intellectual and moral character, and added greatly to the stability of the Papacy securing the return of all church properties in North Central Italy which had been taken by the German Kings. Historians have great praise for him personally and for his administration. He called together the council of 1215 (the Fourth Lateran Council) and produced the Doctrine of Transubtantation. He is regarded as one of the great Popes of Catholicism.

Pope Martin V (1417-1431). His family name was Odocolonna of Rome. He was known as a brilliant and able administrator and followed a determined and vigorous policy to end the great schism that afflicted the church. His efforts were substantially successful, not only in the matter of guiding the church toward unity, but also in continuing to uphold the supremacy of the Papacy. He is credited with bringing an almost hopeless situation under control by his ability and initiative.

Pope Eugenius IV (1431-1447) of Venice, Italy was the nephew of Pope Gregory XII. His family name was Gabriel Condulmer. He was a man of austere habits, was pious, upright, and strongly committed to continuing the policy of unification of the church. His perseverance was rewarded with great success, and his prestige was greatly enhanced to a degree not seen in 200 years. At his death in 1447 his critics accorded and described him as a glorious Pope who despised money and loved virtue. He was fearless and resolute. Physically he was tall, handsome, and majestic. (8 p. 178)

<u>Pope Nicholas V</u> (1447-1455). His name was Tomasso Parentuccelli of Liguria and was the first true Renaissance Pope. He turned Rome into a vast construction site attempting to rebuild and restore 1000 years of devastation. It was said that building and books were his greatest passions. He built or restored nearly 50 churches and conceived the idea of a new St. Peters and a Vatican City. He was possessed of high intelligence and always sought the company of learned men. He spent 30,000 gold florins to restock the Papal Library and employed many "scriptures" to restore and record Papal history. He was also described as a noble person dedicated to glorifying the Papacy.

<u>Pope Paul III</u> (1534-1549). His full name was Alesandro Farnese. He inherited the deep and severe differences in the rise of Luther and the schism which resulted, but he had the courage and foresight to continue the reforming of the church. His problems were monumental, both religious and secular. The problems he faced were beyond the repair by any Pope. However, by the time of his death in 1549, he had rescued the Papacy, preserved its independence, and set a proper course for the future.

<u>Pope Gregory XIII</u> (1572-1585). His name was Ugo Boncompagni of Bologna, Italy. He was gifted, imaginative, intellectual, and taught Canon Law at the University of Bologna. He was also faced with the rapid spread of Protestantism, and was most active and vigorous in his mild diplomatic countermeasures, especially in France. He was successful in regaining much support in keeping Catholicism in France, Austria, and Poland, and was regarded as a victorious counter-reformer.

In the matter of sectarian affairs he is credited, and his name given, to the reform of the calendar, called the Gregorian Calendar which the world has since adopted. It is amazingly accurate with the solar calendar. (Refer to Book I, The Calendar)

<u>Pope Innocent XI</u> (1676-1689). His family name was Odescalchi of Como. He was a strong and highly principled Pope with a very efficient administration. In furthering the reform of the Papacy he greatly improved the treasury, while at the same time provided extensive assistance to the poor, and was awarded the title of Father of the Poor. He was devoted and fervent in his religious duties and outlook. In every respect he strengthened the Holy See and at his passing left it far stronger than it was at the time when he was elected. He was canonized in 1956.

Pope Benedict XIV (1740-1758). His full name was Prospero Lambertini of Bologna. Many historians have the greatest praise for him. Macauly called him the best and wisest of 250 of his predecessors. Walpole wrote that he was loved and esteemed by Papists and Protestants. (8 p. 235) It was said that Pope Benedict XIV was Rome's greatest attraction. He was witty, affable, humane, and pious. In his easygoing manner, he set the pattern for future Popes, and raised the Papacy to a new and higher level of dignity and prestige. His accomplishments were such that at some future and distant time, he will no doubt be a candidate for the title of the "Greatest Pope of all Time."

The principal reason for achieving the summit of this recognition was for his lavish support and expenditures for educational purposes. He founded chairs of study for the most diverse subjects, such as surgery, philosophy, and mathematics. His expansion of the Vatican Library was without precedent. He was also credited with great foresight in rescuing the Church from the many dangers on the horizon.

Pope Pius VII (1800-1823) His name was Barnaba Chiaramonti of Cesena. He was mild of a character, but most formidable in his determination to uphold the vital interests of the church. The need to demonstrate this quality arose in the person of Napoleon Bonaparte, one of the most stubborn opponents of the Papacy in 1000 years. Napoleon, by his alternate use of force and deception, attempted to demoralize and disrupt not only the Pope, but the entire Ecclesiastic community and organization. He was not beyond attempting to wear down the Pontiff by forcing arduous travel in the winter over the Alps and to hopefully cause his death. The famous painting of the scene, wherein Napoleon crowns himself Emperor in the presence of the Pope and the assemblage of nobility, was an example of the extremes to which Napoleon went to demean and demoralize Pope Pius VII. However, nothing worked. Pope Pius VII was an extraordinary person himself. He stood up to Napoleon and confronted and confounded him. His pontificate (23 years and one of the longest) was one crisis after another, and in the end his triumph was heroic. His victory for all to see resulted in continuation of the great Catholic Counter Reformation and revival. This bloodless victory ranked with many previous great events in efforts to enhance Papal prestige throughout the world. Mention must also be made here of Cardinal Consalvi and Cardinal Pacca, Papal Secretary of State. They were two assistants and advisors who were a tower of strength, harmony, and support for the Pope at most critical moments and shared in the ultimate victory. Napoleon, in a reflective moment, referred to him as a "good man and a good priest."

<u>Pope Pius IX</u> (1846-1870) His family name was Mastai. The reign of Pius IX was similar in some respects to that of the aforementioned Pope Pius the VII. The similarity was in the mounting opposition of the political confrontation with the new forces rising in Italy. Radical forces attempting to unite Italy and control the sovereignty of the Papacy were not only encroaching in on the Papacy, but they were also fighting among themselves. This turmoil destabalized every aspect of life, both temporal and spiritual, causing the Pope to be hounded out of Rome into hiding until matters settled down.

Pope Pius IX believed that it was necessary to retain his temporal powers in order to properly carry out his spiritual responsibilities. He believed deeply that he must retain these secular powers because they were confronted from every side by secular pressure. His position was compromised by a liberal element within the Church that felt otherwise. A Vatican Council of 1898 was called which supported the Pope unanimously, a tribute to his leadership. However, with the outbreak of the Franco-Prussian War the opportunity presented itself to the Italian forces whose aim was to unify Italy. Rome became a target and was militarily occupied.

<u>Pope Leo XIII</u> (1878-1903) His full name was Vincenzo Gioacchino Pacci. He was known to be a patient and skillful administrator and determined defender of the independence of the Papacy. During the period when France turned harshly Anti-Clerical, Pope Leo XIII resisted futilely. Laws and obstacles were imposed on the Papacy and its monastic system, including the confiscation of its properties and income.

Pope Leo XIII turned to resolving the social problems involved with the industrial age. His efforts were eminently successful and resulted in the recruitment of a new and vast working class of followers. His encyclicals concerning the doctrines of fairness to the working man were a new page in the employer - employee relationships which defined their responsibilities, and declared that religion should be the basis of their relationship for industrial peace.

He ushered in a new era of social reform which gained worldwide attention. Notwithstanding the restrictions imposed by military occupation of Rome, Pope Leo XIII was generally praised for his courage for preserving the independence of the Papacy, although severely limited to spiritual matters only.

Pope Pius X (1903-1914) His family name was Giuseppe Sarto, of Venice. Pope Pius X was facing, in the early 1900's, a very different world dilemma. World governments were plunging headlong into turmoil and eventually global war. These forces were clearly outside the jurisdiction and influence of the Papacy to solve, and his warnings went unheeded. Pope Pius X then directed his attention to strengthening the internal organization of the church and initiated programs to recodify Canon Law, which had not been attended to for centuries.

He denounced all sides to the coming conflict as a crime against humanity. However, his sincere and heroic efforts to turn the tide of descent into war were swept aside causing him intense personal grief. Catholic countries fighting Catholic countries on such a scale was a calamity of the first magnitude. His health was profoundly affected and it was said to have brought on his early death.

His fervor and piety were recognized to the degree that brought about meriting canonization, which was granted in 1953 under Pope Pius XII, and he was the only Pope canonized after the 13th century. His sanctity was such that two (2) miracles attributed to Pope Pius X were investigated and declared true.

Pope Pius XI (1922-1939) was a native middle-class Italian. He was immediately faced with further loss of independence and was virtually a prisoner of a Fascist Dictatorship. Biding his time, he gradually improved the relationship by taking advantage of public sentiment and weaknesses in the Fascist Regime. At a crucial juncture, he and his Secretary of State, Cardinal Gasperri, negotiated a treaty with a most beneficial and far reaching effect. In essence, the Vatican became an independent state with all the rights appertaining thereto, and in addition, Catholicism became the official religion of Italy. In celebration of this momentous event, the Pope made the public announcement, which was the first Papal appearance after 35 years of seclusion. The Papacy was again part of the world scene and had regained its former status.

Pope Pius XII (1939-1958) His full name was Eugenio Pacelli of Latium, the son of a famous Vatican Lawyer, Filippo Pacelli. (8 p. 285) As Cardinal Pacelli, he was Secretary of State under Pius XI and was selected by Pius XI to be his successor. He was a gifted lawyer, aiding in the codification of Canon Law. He was appointed Secretary of State at the age of twenty-seven and remained in this position until his elevation to the Papacy. He became widely recognized for his ability and experience in international matters, but due to the state of world affairs, the problems he immediately had to face were no different than his predecessor's.

With the savage persecution of Catholics in Spain, France, Germany, and Russia any overt action on the part of the Pope would have resulted in sudden and bloody eclipse of Catholics in the countries confronted. In essence, the Papacy had to remain rigidly neutral to survive for the long term and to protect Catholics against totalitarian abuse. Private objections to the heads of State were continually voiced, but public confrontations had to be avoided other than to press for a just peace and for cessation of oppression of the civil populations. To support this policy, he formed the Vatican Radio system which Germany demanded be shut down, but was refused. When his efforts began to be recognized in a positive sense, President Roosevelt appointed an ambassador to the Vatican who was to represent the President personally. The situation in Europe was fluid and extremely dangerous at every turn of events. Germany and Russia, bitter enemies, suddenly signed a pact of non-aggression; then after they partitioned Poland, Germany turned and invaded Russia. France had collapsed, England had its back to the wall and was calling for American intervention.

In this maelstrom, to carry out the mission of the Papacy, martyrdom of Catholicism by a paranoid dictator was obviously not the answer. To raise one's head would surely get it shot off. For the long term, a measure of neutrality was necessary to allow the totalitarians to wear themselves out. While Pope Pius XII has been criticized in some narrow-quarters, his policy survived the momentous events that followed. It must be remembered that after the fall of Mussolini, and the occupation of Rome by anti-Papist Germany, the entire Papacy could have been obliterated at any moment.

Therefore, their tightrope walk through this period was an exercise in a combination of actions and diplomacy. It is unfortunate that this criticism is still voiced in some quarters, but according to one Jewish source, the Catholic Church saved some 400,000 Jews. It saved more Jewish lives than all other churches, religious institutions and rescue organizations put together.

With the defeat of the Axis nations, Communism filled the void and spread throughout the world including Italy. The Pope proclaimed absolute opposition to this Godless Society even to forbidding Catholics everywhere in the world to cooperate or vote for it.

Pope Pius XI and Pope Pius XII, by threading their way through a period as perilous for the world as any in history, played a major part in destablizing Russian Communism. They preserved the future of everyone with a substantially reduced threat of worldwide calamity.

There is no question that the people of the world are in debt to these great and dedicated men. Their religious name, "Pius," aptly describes them: "Dutiful regard for religious obligations."

<u>Pope John XXIII</u> (1958-1963) His full name was Angelo Roncali from Bergamo. He called into session the second Vatican Council to face the problems of the post-war world. The more pressing problems were the reunification of Christians, examination of the relationship between the state and the individual in the modern world, and problems arising due to the theoretical atheistic Marxism and practical Communism that was promised to be responsive to the individual. He allowed Catholics to vote for communists if they wished thus reversing the prohibition laid down by Pope Pius XII.

Pope John XXIII died before the work of the Council was completed. Nevertheless, the Council went on to direct the Catholic Church to the vigorous task of urging governments to respect religious, economic, and political rights of the individual, which in effect, was a new philosophy.

It is said that his leadership placed the Church in the mainstream of the new modern world and in a better position to cope with the irreligious views and the materialism which was on the rise throughout the world. The new church was to be a recognized force in the world for peace.

SAINTS - THE HONOR ROLL OF CHRISTIANITY
PREFACE TO SAINTS

The first saints were all martyrs. A martyr was regarded and accorded the highest respect and esteem in Christianity. They were "Sainted" automatically by their sacrifice and not by recognition or formal action by the church. The date of his martyrdom was the date reserved for honoring that particular saint.

Many churches were founded on the name of a special saint and on whom the church would call upon in its prayers. The tradition began very early in Christian history as Christians gathered for worship at the tomb of the martyrs in the catacombs. Often, the church building was the repository of the tomb and remains of the martyr, or most often, contained a relic of the saint.

It should be noted here that the church did not advocate any form of saint worship, but only to be called upon as mediators for placing petitions before God. He was considered "influential," but nothing more. It should also be noted that the church did not encourage martyrdom, but in fact, opposed it. Certain cults arose seeking martyrdom which was vigorously opposed by the church and declared it a heresy. Uninvited martyrdom was saintly, but not if it was sought after. Furthermore, the conduct of that cult, Montanism, endangered everyone and was not the preferred way to spread the Gospel. Piety and good works, yes, but suicide, no.

Saints were very often role models for the devout Christian and many sought to emulate them. The lifestyle of a saint also inspired many to follow their example.

HONOR ROLL OF ITALIAN SAINTS

St. Paulinus (726-804) was born in Frioli and through self-education rose to being appointed Patriarch of Aquileia. He worked diligently in all aspects of church doctrine and missionary vocations.

St. Agnes (? - 304) was a young Roman woman who devoted her short life to piety and prayer. She was martyred for her faith and buried near Via Nomentana, Rome. The Christian Emperor later built a church in her honor.

St. Thomas Aquinas (1225-1274) was born in Aquino, Italy and is regarded as the greatest scholastic Theologian of the Middle Ages. His works form the basis of Roman Catholic Theology. (Refer to section on "Theologians")

St. John Bosco (1815-1888) was born in Turin and dedicated his life to caring for young children. He founded the Oratory, the Salesian Society of St. Francis deSales, and the Daughters of Mary Help of Christians.

St. Angela Merici (1474-1540) was born in Desenzano and founded schools for young girls. She further devoted her life to saving souls and founded the congregation of Ursulines in Brescia, the first teaching order in the church.

St. Agatha (?-251) was born in Sicily of noble birth and was tortured and martyred for her faith on the orders of pagan Senator Quintanius.

St. Jerome of Stridonium (345-420) was born of Italian heritage near Venice. Early in his adult life he took a vow of celibacy and withdrew to a private life of prayer and contemplation. He was a highly gifted individual and his council was eagerly sought. (Refer to the details on pages 86 and 114.)

St. Apollonia (?-248) was believed to have been born in Rome and was a deaconess of the early church ministering to the sick and the poor. She was brutally tortured by a mob of Pagans and martyred for her faith.

St. Scholastica (485?-543) was born in Nursia, the sister of St. Benedict, and was a devout and pious nun. She founded a monastery of nuns near her brother at Monte Casino spending her life in prayer, study, and good works. After she died, her brother, Benedict buried her in a tomb in Monte Casino that he had prepared for himself.

St. Catherine deRicci (1522-1589) was born in Florence and at an early age lived in a convent with her aunt, Sister Louisa de Ricci. She was regarded as highly intelligent and was given substantial responsibilities while still a young nun. Learned men often sought her counsel.

St. Valentine (?-270?) was a young Roman priest who was martyred for his faith. The ancient custom of boys drawing names of girls in honor of a Pagan Goddess, but later changed to names of saints, was attributed to him.

St. Conrad of Piacenza (1290-1351) was born in Piacenza, Italy. As a result of a tragic event that was his fault, he made what financial restitution he could and then entered a Franciscan Order. He spent the remaining years of his life caring for the sick. His wife, as her penance, entered the convent of Poor Clares devoting her life to prayer.

St. Peter Damian (1007-1072) was born in Ravenna and was one of the more illustrious religious individuals of the time. He was a monk of the Benedictine Order and was also its Abbot, later becoming Bishop of Ostia. He worked closely with St. Gregory VII for reform of the church and was later honored with the Degree, Doctor of the Church.

St. Gabriel (1838-1862) was born in Assisi and his birthname was Francis Possenti. As a young man at the Jesuit College of Spoleto, he was recognized for his sanctity, self-denial, piety, and was held in great esteem by his fellow students. He died of tuberculosis at the age of twenty-four.

St. Paul of the Cross (1694-1775) was born in Ovada, near Genoa and displayed fervent piety at an early age. He diligently applied himself to forming a congregation which was approved by Pope Benedict XIV. He also founded two monasteries, one at Obitello and the other in Rome. The habit worn by the monks resembled those of the Passionists of today. They were devoted to missionary work.

St. John Joseph of the Cross (1650-1734) was born on the Island of Ischia, Bay of Naples and at the age of sixteen entered the Franciscan Order of Strictest Observance. He became a priest and founded a monastery in Piedmont, Italy. His entire life was spent laboring for the improvement of his order and training of novices. He was especially virtuous and disciplined.

St. Perpetua and St. Felicitas (?-203) were living in the Italian colony of Carthage and both were martyred for their faith. Perpetua kept a diary of her suffering and life in the dungeon. Her executioner was unnerved by her calmness as she instructed him in where he should use his sword.

St. Frances of Rome (1384-1440) was born in Rome. She was a devout Christian and founded the Oblate Congregation of Tor Di Specchi.

St. Dominic Savio (1842-1857) was born in Riva. He was a pupil of John Bosco, known for his religious fervor, and founded the company of the Immaculate Conception.

St. Patrick (389-461) was the son of Italians, Calpurnius and Conchessa. He went on to become Bishop of Palladius, Ireland and was recognized for his success in converting much of the population.

St. Francis of Paola (1416-1508) was born in Paola, Calabria and spent most of his life in prayer and counseling others. He founded the Order of Minims in 1474 and went to France where he converted King Louis XI.

St. Marcellinis of Carthage (360-413) was born to poor parents in the Italian colony at Carthage. He was Secretary of State to Emperor Honorius, but was later accused of rebellion and was martyred.

St. Gemma Galgani (1878-1903) was born near Lucca and spent her life in prayer, pursuing her religious vocation for the benefit of others.

St. Julius (285-352) was a Roman and became the Bishop of Rome as well as Pope Julius I. He is credited with establishing the Papacy as an international figure.

St. Tiburtius, Valerius and Maximus were third century Roman soldiers martyred for their faith and they are buried in Rome.

St. Justin Martyr (100?-165) was not of Italian ancestry. He was an early philosopher and writer whose works are still in existence. (Refer to section under "Theologians") He was the founder of the First School of Christian Philosophy and was martyred by rival elements in 165. (Included here to stress importance of theology)

St. Apollonius (110-186) was born in Rome and was martyred for his steadfast faith after an eloquent defense of Christianity in a speech before Pagan senators.

St. Marcellinus (300?-374) was born in the Italian colony of Carthage. He became a great preacher converting the whole city of Embron, near the Alps, where he built an oratory.

St. Zita (1205-1278) was born in Lucca. She was the sister of a Cistercian nun and the niece of Griziano the Hermit. She spent her life performing good works, counseling and feeding the poor.

St. Catherine of Siena (1347-1380) was the daughter of an Italian tradesman (Marynoll Missal P, 860) and became one of the most renown women of her age. Her accomplishments were many, and substantial, including becoming Counselor to Pope Gregory XI. She was awarded the title Doctor of the Church, and died at age 33.

St. Pius V (Pope) (1504-1572) was born to poor parents. His full name was Michael Ghislieri and early in life became a priest and teacher. He is credited with completing a leading part in Catholic Reformation of the Church.

St. Francis di Girolamo (1642-1716). He was born in Taranto and worked most of his life preaching and conducting charitable missions. He is the Patron Saint of Naples, Italy.

St. Benedict (480-543) was born in Nursia, Italy. In 529 he founded the Great Monastery at Monte Casino and established the Benedictine Rule that was followed by many later monastic orders. His sister, St. Scholastica, became the first Benedictine nun at an Abbey founded nearby. (Refer to more details under heading of "Monasteries and Orders.") He was also accorded the Degree of Doctor of the Church.

St. John Gualbert (1010-1073) was born in Florence and was the founder of the Order of Vallombra. He established the strict rule that no indigent person should ever be sent away without assistance.

St. Bonaventure (1221-1274) was born in Bagnorea, Tuscanny Italy. He studied under Thomas Aquinas, and was the author of many works, including the "Life of St. Francis." He also received the degree of Doctor of the Church.

St. Arsenius (354-449) was born in Rome and was a monk tutor to the sons of Emperor Theodosius. He was the author of the famous forty-four maxims to live by. (For example "I have often been sorry for having spoken, but never for having held my tongue.")

St. Lawrence of Brindisi (1560-1619) was born in Brindisi. He performed a remarkable feat by leading an army of Christians against an army of Turks in a crucial battle with only a Crucifix held high above his head. He was victorious and saved Europe from Turkish domination. Through his diligence and perseverance he received the degree of Doctor of the Church.

St. Alphonsus of Liguori (1696-1775) was born in Marianella, Naples and was the founder of the Congregation of the Most Holy Redeemer. Their objective was to work to redeem the most abandoned of society. Through his dedication and study, he received the degree of Doctor of the Church.

St. Eusebius of Vercelli (315-370) was born in Sardinia, Italy, but lived in Rome from infancy until he became Bishop in 340. He was an advisor to Emperor Constantine and was the author of the book "History of the Church." (From Christ to Constantine - the first 300 years.) Remarkably, the book is still in print and is currently sold in bookstores.

St. Sixtus and Companians (210-258) was a Pope and was martyred along with St. Felicissimus, St. Agapitus, and four deacons.

St. Cajetan (1480-1547) was born in Vincenza. He founded the Order of Theatines, and while a Cardinal, was highly regarded for his diplomatic ability.

St. Romanus (225-258) was a Roman soldier who was inspired to conversion by the persecution of St. Lawrence, and was martyred the day before the Martyrdom of St. Lawrence.

St. Lawrence (230-258) ministered to the poor and was martyred for refusing to give the church's treasuries to the Emperor. He gave them to the poor instead.

St. Clare (1193-1253) was born in Assisi. She founded the Order of Poor Clares or Second Order of St. Francis. She was dedicated to helping the poor and was known for her piety and good works.

St. Euplus (275-304?) was born in Catania, Sicily. He was martyred for openly professing his Christian faith and was executed with the book of the Gospels tied to his body.

St. Pontinis (185-235) was born in Rome. He was an early Pope (230-235) and was martyred for defending his faith.

St. Hippolytus (170-235) was born in Rome and was a priest at the time he was martyred together with St. Pontinis. He was an early theologian, writing the earliest known commentary on scripture.

St. Pius X (1835-1914) was born in Treviso near Venice. His full name was Giuseppe Melchiorre Sarto. He was elevated to the Papacy in 1903 and worked tirelessly to divert the coming of World War I. He also had a special interest in promoting frequent communion and avoiding the evils associated with modernism.

St. Monica (333-387) was the mother of St. Augustine of Hippo. By her faith, piety, example, and perseverance, she led St. Augustine (her son) to the Christian Faith.

St. Augustine of Hippo (354-430) was born of Italian heritage (son of St. Monica) in the Italian community of Hippo, North Africa. Through the efforts of his mother and St. Ambrose of Milan, he became one of the most important theologians and Doctors of the Church. At his death in 430 he was the Bishop of Hippo. (Refer to more details under "Theologians.")

St. Peter Chrysologus (406-450) was born in Imola. He was known as an eloquent preacher and was highly regarded for his piety and for helping the unfortunate and poor. He became the Archbishop of Ravenna and was made Doctor of the Church. (He was known as The Man of Golden Speech.)

St. John I (468?-526) was born in Tuscany and became Pope in 523. He was known for his diplomatic ability and was credited with bringing about the reconciliation of the Eastern and Western Churches. He was later martyred under the Gothic Emperor Theodoric.

St. Gregory The Great (540-604) was born in Rome. He attained the highest honors and recognition as Pope, Theologian, Doctor of the Church, and for his missionary efforts. (Refer to sections on Popes and Theologians.)

St. Rosalia (1102-1160) was born in Palermo, Sicily. She became deeply religious and dedicated herself to prayer, counseling and good works.

St. Nicholas of Tolentino (1245-1306) was born in Fermo and dedicated his life to prayer, counseling and good works.

St. Robert Bellarmine (1542-1621) was born in Montepulciano and was an outstanding scholar and writer. He became a Bishop, Cardinal, and Doctor of the Church. (Refer also to "Theologians" for more details.)

St. Joseph of Cupertino (1603-1663) was born in Nardo. He was known for his fervent dedication to prayer, good works, and work among the poor.

St. Januarius (275-305) was born in Naples and became Bishop of Benvenuto, Italy. He was condemned to be thrown to the animals in the arena, but miraculously none of the animals touched him. He was later martyred and is the Patron Saint of Naples.

St. Constantius (520-560) was a layman born in Ancona and was the sacristan of the Cathedral of St. Stephen in Ancona. He was deeply devout and dedicated his life to prayer, good works, and helping the poor and sick.

St. Pacifico of San Severino (1653-1721) was born in San Severino. After his ordination he spent his life ministering to people of the mountain village and helping the poor.

St. Francis of Assisi (1181-1226) was born in Assisi, Italy and was the founder of the Franciscan Order of Little Brothers, which became one of the world's largest orders. (Refer to more details under Monasteries and Orders.)

St. John Leonardi (1541-1609) was born in Lucca. As a priest, he devoted his life to serving the youth and restoring church discipline. He was the founder of the Clerics Regular of the Mother of God.

St. Callistus (170?-222) was born in Rome and early in life was a slave. He lived a story-book life rising from his lowly status to that of Pope Calixtus I, and then martyrdom.

St. Gregory VII (1010?-1085) was born in Tuscany, Italy. He led a lifelong effort as Pope to establish independence of the church from secular rulers.

St. Gerard Majella (1726-1755) was born in Muro and became a Redemptorist Priest, devoting his life to works of counseling and charity.

St. Gaudentius of Brescia (350-410) was born in Brescia was a highly acclaimed preacher and writer. Ten of his famous written sermons still exist to this day. He was elected Bishop of Brescia and was dedicated to inspiring the faithful to imitate Jesus.

St. Charles Borromeo (1538-1584) was born in the area of Lake Maggiore near Milan. He became the Archbishop of Milan and was a tireless worker for reform of the Church. He founded the Vatican Academy for Literary Work and composed the Roman Catechism. (Refer to more detail following this section.)

St. Sylvia (510-594?) was born in Sicily and was the mother of Pope Gregory I The Great. She was devoutly religious, dedicated to good works and furthering the teaching of the Gospel.

St. Leo I The Great (402-461) was born in Tuscany, Italy and was one of the only two Popes granted the title "The Great." (See Section on Popes and additional details.)

St. Frances Xavier Cabrini (1850-1917) was born in Lombardy, Italy. She became a school teacher and founded the Missionary Sisters of the Sacred Heart for poor children. She came to America and continued her work in founding schools, hospitals, and orphanages, and became the first American citizen to be canonized.

St. Cecilia (140-161) was born in Rome, was a devout Christian and was recognized for converting Tiburtius to Christianity. (He was the brother of Emperor Valerian.) She was martyred for her faith and an image of her body is displayed where it was found-in a burial nitch in the Roman catacombs.

St. James of the March (1391-1476) His birth name was James Gangala and he was born in Ancona. He worked unceasingly for conversions and it was said he converted 50,000 heretics to Christianity. He was also an inspiring speaker. (He was the Billy Graham of his day.)

St. Saturninus (215-257) was born in Rome and converted many unbelievers to Christianity. He was martyred in Gaul for refusing to offer sacrifices to the Emperor and to Pagan Gods.

St. Florence (335-366) was born in Asia Minor, daughter of Roman colonists. She was devoted to prayer and good works throughout her life.

St. Bibiana (350?-370) was the daughter of a Roman soldier (Flavian) and Dafrosa (his wife) She and her parents were martyred for refusing to renounce their faith.

St. Lucy (?-304) was born in Syracuse, Italy and dedicated her life to prayer and pious living. She was martyred for her faith under the reign of Diocletian.

St. Gatian (? -?). Was born to Roman parents but lived most of his life in Tours, Gaul. He became Bishop, and was famous for his preaching and many conversions.

St. Sylvester (248-335) was born in Rome and as Pope Sylvester I, worked vigorously for unification of church doctrine.

St. Juliana of Falconieri (1270-1341) was born in Florence, Italy and was the niece of Alcessio Falconieri, one of the seven founders of the Order of Servites. (Refer to Section on Monasteries and Orders)

St. Prisca (?250?) was born in Rome. She was devoted to prayer, a pious life, and was martyred for her faith. Her remains are buried in the Church on Aventine Hill in Rome.

St. Alexis (Third Century?) was of Roman heritage and spent his life performing good works, prayer, and begging for the poor.

St. Peter of Verona (1205-1252) was born in Verona and was known as an outstanding preacher. His conversions were so numerous that he was marked for assassination by heretics. He was attacked and died writing the Creed on the ground in his own blood.

St. Saturninus and 48 Companions (Approx. 304) was a priest from an Italian colony in Abitina, North Africa and was martyred for defending his faith, refusing to make sacrifices and devotions to Pagan Gods.

Ss. Nereus, Achilleus and Pancras (First Century) were Roman soldiers martyred for their faith and are buried on Via Ardentina in Rome. The carved bust of Achilleus is the earliest known sculpture of a martyr known to Christendom.

St. Rita Cascia (1381-1487) was born in Spoleto. After the death of her husband and children, she entered a Franciscan convent in Cascia devoting her remaining life to prayer and charity.

St. John Baptist DeiRossi (1698-1764) was born in Voltaggio and for much of his life devoted his labors to ministering to the poor of Campagna, Italy. As a priest he spent many hours preparing the faithful for the sacraments and at the same time became a great preacher. He labored continually and literally wore out his body performing his mission.

St. Mary Magdalen de Pazzi (1566-1607) was born in Florence and given to prophecy. She was devoted to prayer, penance, and labored to reform the church.

St. Philip Neri (1515-1595) was born in Florence. In his priesthood he became active in philosophy and theology. He established the Confraternity of the Blessed Trinity in 1548 and founded the Oratory in 1575.

St. Augustine of Canterbury (550-604) was one of the Italian monks sent to England by Pope Gregory I to convert the Britons and he became the first Archbishop of Canterbury. (Refer also to section on "Popes" -Gregory I - The Great.)

Ss. Marcellinus and Peter (Second Century Italian martyrs) Marcellinus was a priest and Peter was an exorcist. Both were imprisoned for their faith and condemned. However, while in prison they converted their executioner who became a Christian. Their names are preserved in the Roman Canon Eucharistic Prayer I.

St. Francis Caracciolo (1563-1608) was born in Naples with the baptismal name of Ascanio, but after becoming a priest changed it to Francis in honor of St. Francis of Assisi. He labored among the poor and sick and to those in the prisons. He was co-founder (with John Adorno) of the Order of the Clerics Minors.

St. Guy Vignotelli (1185-1245) was born in Cortona and after meeting with St. Francis of Assisi, he became a priest and follower of St. Francis. He was known as very devout and humble. Several miracles were attributed to him.

St. Methodius (779-847) was born to a noble family in Syracuse, Sicily, but spent his life in Constantinople where he later became patriarch. He labored long and fearlessly against improper church practices and instituted the Feast of Orthodoxy which is still observed in Byzantine Churches to this day.

St. Gregory Barbarigo (1625-1697) was born to a noble family in Venice and was recognized as a highly intelligent youth. He went on to become a priest and Bishop of Bergamo. After he was elevated to Cardinal, he worked resolutely to carry out the reforms of the Council of Trent.

St. Romuald (956-1027) was born in Ravenna. He was a monk and later became Abbot of a Benedictine Monastery. He was known for his prayer and overcoming temptations.

St. Aloysius Gonzaga (1568-1591) was born in Castiglione, Bressica, Italy the son of a Marquis. He entered the Order of the Society of Jesus, but died before final ordination at the age of twenty-four. He was known for his work of charity and ministering to the sick. He is the Patron Saint of the Young.

St. Anthelm (1107-1178) was born in the area of Savoy, Italy to a noble family. He was highly intelligent, and was given the advantage of a good education. He became a monk and later became the Prior of the Order of Grande Chartruse, and was credited with improving and expanding it. Other monasteries followed his plans and programs and he later became Bishop of Belley, France.

St. Bernardino Realino (1530-1616) was born on the Isle of Capri and after receiving a degree in law, he assumed a high civil position in Naples. He became a priest in the Society of Jesus and devoted himself to serving the poor and youthful people of Naples and Lecce, Italy. His deep devotion to saving souls and works of charity were widely recognized. He was also the rector of the Jesuit College in Lecce.

St. Anthony Zaccaria (1502-1539) was born in Cremona, studied medicine and became a physician at age twenty-two. He became a priest while continuing to practice medicine and devoted his labors to everyone. He founded a community called the Angelicals and also founded the Order of Clerics Regular of St. Paul. He labored steadily and died at the early age of thirty-seven.

St. Maria Goretti (1890-1902) was born in Ancona and was devout in her faith. She helped her mother raise her younger brothers and sisters after the death of her father. She was mortally wounded by an attacker, but before her death she prayed for him and forgave him for his crime. Upon his release from prison (after twenty-five years), in restitution for his crime, he begged forgiveness and devoted the remainder of his life to religious causes as a Capuchin lay brother.

<u>Seven Holy Brothers</u> were martyred in Rome about 162 A.D. before the eyes of their mother (widow, Symphorosa) all of whom refused to recant their faith.

<u>Ss. Rufina and Secunda</u> were daughters of a distinguished Roman family who were martyred about 260 A.D. for their faith and refusing to marry pagan suitors.

<u>St. Veronica Giuliani</u> (1660-1727) was born in Mercatello. At an early age she displayed devout religious characteristics and entered the convent of Poor Clares. Her deep and devout faith later manifested itself each Good Friday by wounds of the Stigmata.

<u>St. Augustine of Hippo</u> (354-430) Refer to section Important Early Saints who were not Popes. (p. 121)

<u>St. Ambrose of Milan</u> (339-397) Refer to section Important Early Saints who were not Popes. (p. 121)

<u>St. Jerome of Stridonium</u> (345-420) Refer to section Important Early Saints who were not Popes. (p. 86) also (p. 121)

<u>St. Francis de Sales</u> (1550?-1622) was born in the province of Savoy, the child of an aristocratic family. He was noted for his many conversions, writings, and leading role in The Catholic Reformation. Together with St. Jane de Chantal, he founded the Order of the Visitation.

<u>St. Martina</u> (200? -228) was born in Rome and consecrated her life to helping the poor. She gave away all her possessions and refused to renounce her faith. She was martyred in 228 A.D.

<u>St. Andrew of Corsini</u> (1300?-1373) was born in Florence to a noble family. He entered the Carmelite order and worked diligently and anonymously to help the poor, especially those who were too ashamed to ask for assistance. He became bishop of Fiesole, and helped mend errors occurring in the church.

St. Faustinus (? - 121) was born in Brescia and became active in openly preaching the Christian Religion. He refused to renounce his faith and was martyred along with St. Jovita.

St. Jovita (? - 121) was born in Brescia and was a friend and associate of St. Faustinus. He was martyred for his faith at the same time with St. Faustinus.

St. John of Capistrano (1386 - 1460) was born in Capistrano, Naples, Italy. He became a lawyer and was governor of Perugia. After entering the Franciscan order, he went on to evangelize Italy, France, Germany, Austria, Hungary, and Poland. He was also a leader in the Crusades against the Turks.

St. Antonius (1389-1459) was born in Florence. He was christened as Anthony, but was called Antonius because of his small stature. He was active in the Dominican Order in his charitable work for the poor, giving away everything he owned. He became archbishop of Florence and because of his unending efforts to help the poor, he was referred to as "the father of the poor."

St. Domitilla (First Century) Was the niece of one of the Consuls of Rome at that time. She was martyred for her faith at the approximate time of Ss. Nereus and Achilleus. They were praetorian soldiers who guarded the emperor and were converted to Christianity and martyred.

St. Boniface (500 - 530?) was born in Rome and although he was not a member of a religious community, he was recognized for his kindness to the poor. He was martyred when he went to the aid of a group of Christians who were being attacked by heretics, and was himself killed by them.

St. Ubald (1129 - 1189?) was born in Gubbio, and his birth name was Ubald Baldassini. He became the Bishop of Gubbio serving for thirty (30) years and because he influenced rival groups to avoid violence, he was known as the peacemaker. He once met the Emperor outside Gubbio and persuaded him to space the city from violence.

St. Venantius (250 - 265) was born in Camerino and was martyred when he was only 15. He was steadfast in his faith, through his tortures, until his death. His example was said to have resulted in the conversion of many pagans to Christianity.

St. Peter Celestine (1221 - 1296) was born in the Tuscan hills of Northern Italy and at an early age retired to live in seclusion and prayer. Many came to receive his council and his reputation became widespread which became the foundation of the Celestine Order. He was elevated to Pope, but in his humility, he resigned after only five (5) months, feeling himself incapable of performing administrative duties.

St. Bernardine of Siena (1380 - 1444) was born near Siena and became a priest in the Franciscan Order. He was extremely active his entire life, traveling all over Italy preaching and providing counseling. He was credited with converting thousands of souls to Christianity.

St. Felix I (250? - 274) was born in Rome where he lived and served the church his entire life. He became Pope in 269 A.D. during a period of heretical uprisings and disturbances. He was firm in his administration and condemned the heresy of the Bishop of Antioc thus avoiding further separation of East and West at that time. He was later martyred under the reign of Emperor Aurelian in 274.

St. Anthony of Padua (1195 - 1231) was by birth of Portuguese ancestry but was born, (Padua) educated, and influenced by his Italian environment. He was therefore regarded as a product of Italy. His superior talent as a preacher and his knowledge of Scripture became widely recognized. Pope Gregory IX referred to him as the "Ark of the Testament." Because of his profound depth of Scriptural knowledge and teachings, he was granted the title Doctor of the Church.

Ss. Vitus, Modestus, Crescentia (9th. Century?) were born in southern Italy. The dates are uncertain, although it was some time during the middle ages. Modestus was a tutor and Crescentia a nurse of St. Vitus. All were martyred for their faith in Lucania.

St. William (1085 - 1142) was born in the northern province of Piedmont. He lived a life of seclusion and prayer. His reputation grew and he drew many followers who sought his council. He later founded the Congregation of the Williamites, under the rules of St. Benedict, and they dedicated themselves to the Blessed Virgin.

St. John of Rome (? - 362) was born in Rome and was martyred for his faith after refusing to submit to Emperor Julian. He was martyred with his brother, St. Paul of Rome. He first gave all of his possessions to the poor.

St. Paul of Rome (? - 362) was born in Rome and martyred for his faith after refusing to submit to Emperor Julian. He was martyred with his brother, St. John of Rome. He first gave all of his possessions to the poor.

St. Camillus de Lellis (1550 ? - 1620 ?) was believed to have been born in Rome. He was a war veteran, became a priest, and devoted his entire life to nursing the sick and victims of the plague. He organized hospitals and the religious society, Ministers of the Sick. He has since been called the Red Cross Saint and is the patron saint of the sick. He also founded the order of Clerics Regular for the sick.

St. Symphorosa (? - 162) was the mother of the Seven Holy Brothers who were martyred for their faith in 162.

St. Jerome Emiliani (1481 -1537) was born in Venice of a prominent Patrician family. After being captured in war and put in a dungeon, he escaped under what he termed as miraculous circumstances after prayer to the Blessed Virgin. He dedicated his life to works of charity and the care of orphans and the sick. He founded orphanages and hospitals and became a priest. In 1528 he founded the Order of Clerics Regular of Somascha dedicated to the continuation of his work. He died in 1537 from disease contracted while attending the sick. He is the Patron Saint of Orphans.

St. Christina (285 ? -307) was born in Tuscany and was dedicated to her faith and to helping the poor. She destroyed the idols in her father's home and distributed his gold and belongings to the poor. She was punished when she was turned over to her persecutors and was martyred in 307.

St. Nazarius and Celsus (50 ? -68) were friends and companions, both born in Rome. They traveled all over Italy preaching their faith in Christianity, and were martyred by Pagans in Milan in 68.

St. Victor I (135 ? -198) was born in an Italian colony in North Africa and was elected Pope in approximately 190 A.D. He was martyred under the reign of Emperor Septimus Severus in 198 A.D.

St. Innocent I (350 ? -417) Was a Third Century Pope who was born in the province of Tuscany and became the Pope in 402 A.D. He was steadfast in preserving the faith, according to the scriptures, and to urging the faithful to avoid heresy.

St. Susanna (268 ? - 288) was a young Roman maiden who refused to marry the son of Emperor Diocletian. She wished to devote her life to the practice of her faith, but was martyred instead.

St. Cassian (285 ? -320) was born in Imola and became a respected Christian schoolmaster in his home city. The governor of his province ordered that he be arrested and then tortured. He was martyred for his faith.

St. Agapitus (260 -275) was born in Palestrina, Italy and because of his profession of faith in Christianity, he was thrown into the arena with wild animals. When the animals refused to harm him, the Emperor ordered him killed. A Roman official who witnessed this amazing display of faith was moved to conversion to Christianity.

St. Philip Benizi (1233 -1294) was born in Florence and became a priest in the Order of Servites. He traveled extensively in Europe winning many conversions and helping restore peace in war torn Italy.

St. Zephyrinus (145 -217) was born in Rome and developed a strong defense of the divinity of Christ during the period of his priesthood. He was elevated to Pope in 199 A.D. and through his strong adherence to his faith and scripture, overcame the heretics who threatened him.

St. Lawrence Justinian (1380 -1455) was born in Venice to a noble and deeply religious family. After experiencing a vision, he became a priest in the Canons Regular of St. George and later the Bishop of Venice. His fervent prayer, preaching and his example of piety overcame civil and spiritual travails of his time.

St. Eustace (78 ? - 118) was born in Rome and became a distinguished Roman official. He, his wife, and two sons were converted to Christianity under what he believed were miraculous circumstances. In 118 A.D. he and his family were martyred for refusing to sacrifice to false gods.

St. Chrysanthus and Daria (? -283) were born in Rome to noble families. After their conversion to Christianity, they were denounced and martyred by being buried alive.

St. Andrew of Avellino (? - 1390 ?) was born in Naples and became a distinguished lawyer. He gave up his practice and became a priest in the Order of Theatines. He served as director with great success, and was recognized as a needed reformer.

St. Erasmus A.K.A. St. Elmo(? -? Second Century) was born in the province of Campania, and became the Bishop of Formiae, Compania. He is the Patron Saint of Sailors. The occurrence of light from electrical storms glowing high on the masts of ships at sea is referred to as St. Elmo's Light.

FURTHER DETAILS ON ST. CHARLES BORROMEO

St. Charles Borromeo (1539-84)

He was born near Milan and was the nephew of Pope Pius IV. Today, he would have been called a "workaholic". Borromeo was a tireless worker, deeply pious, dedicated to improving the Church, and to helping young priests. He founded several seminaries and assisted in reforming monasteries to increase the effectiveness of their mission. He also inaugurated a number of schools for the poor, teaching both secular and religious subjects. He established several homes for beggars who were provided with advocates in the event they became involved with the law.

He was constantly at work, never denying anyone in need of assistance. It was said he worked himself to death at the age of forty-six. He was canonized in 1610.

IMPORTANT EARLY SAINTS WHO WERE NOT POPES

There were many early saints of Italian heritage who, although highly regarded and influential, were not elevated to the Papacy. The following are three who attained recognition as being particularly outstanding in the early years of Christianity.

St. Augustine of Hippo (354-430) was of Italian heritage born in the Italian colony of Hippo, North Africa and later became a dominant figure in the early Christian period. (Refer to previous section under Theologians for more details.) He was also honored with the degree Doctor of the Church and it is also worthy of note that his mother was later canonized as St. Monica.

St. Ambrose of Milan (339-397) was born to noble Roman parents and gained a widespread reputation as being an outstanding preacher, administrator, and politician. He effectively used his abilities to influence emperors, improving their attitude toward the treatment of Christians. It was Ambrose, as Bishop of Milan, who was instrumental in the conversion of Augustine of Hippo. One of his innovations was that he first introduced community singing in church. He was also awarded the honor and title Doctor of the Church. (Refer also to section on Theologians.)

St. Jerome of Stridonium (345-420) was born of Italian heritage near Venice, Italy. He was not recognized as a classical theologian but he was recognized as the most learned Biblical Scholar of all time. He translated the Bible and other religious works into Latin, a twenty-one year effort. It is known as the Vulgate Bible. He was also honored with the title Doctor of the Church. (For more details refer to section on Theologians.)

There were many others of Italian heritage not included here since their records are lost in the dimness of history. Records were more reliable for those born on the Italian mainland, but many were born in the far reaches of the Roman Empire. During the hey-day of the Empire, given the facility of travel, Italian colonies sprung up from Africa to Asia Minor. "There had been colonies in Constantinople for a long time and throughout the Empire." (23 p. 115)

INFLUENCES ON THE SPREAD OF CHRISTIANITY
FROM OUTSIDE THE CHURCH

Art, music, literature, and architecture were also influential in the proselytizing of Christianity.

The artist, or his patron, provided visual supports and emphasis to the spoken word. Mosaics were believed to be the earliest visual creations depicting religious scenes and characters. The fact that mosaics are more durable probably accounts for the longevity of this category of religious art. The vast majority of ancient art no longer exists except in mosaic form. Furthermore, much of it was carried off during the invasions and the sacking of Rome. The same is true with very early sculpture where religious scenes or ceremonies were made part of an object, monument, or tomb. All of these art forms were very popular mediums used by Italian artists.

As Christianity developed throughout the centuries and church buildings were allowed to be built (after the Edict Of Milan by Emperor Constantine in 313 A.D.), architecture was added to the Christian art form. (Prior to this, religious ceremonies had to be held in secret or in private homes or in the catacombs.) Buildings could now be designed, inspired by religious feeling, and used for meditation. Preaching with good acoustics was impossible in the catacombs. Furthermore, religious articles could now remain in the church instead of in the home where their discovery could result in severe punishment or even a death sentence, prior to the Edict of Milan.

The invention of the arch, dome and cement by Roman architects and builders allowed for a new type of structure. The dome was an inspirational design created to cover a revered hallowed spot or object such as a tomb. This design was later used everywhere in Christian structures of all types, including monasteries.

Now that paintings and other less durable objects could be protected from the elements, the interiors were decorated with a visual story of the New Testament. Every other art form then flourished, encouraged by the church and wealthy patrons, creating new inspirational mediums.

This was a gradual process over many centuries, but nonetheless it raised the level of sensitivity. Now, one could not only hear the words of the Gospel but also visualize it. In the 20th Century, we now stand in awe of these marvelous creations in paintings, sculpture and architecture.

We can well imagine the impact of this tremendous display on those who viewed it for the first time.

Music was added to give emphasis to the ceremony and prayers thus creating hymns. Pope Gregory I The Great encouraged music at Mass which, when sung, was known as the Gregorian Chant. Later, prominent musical artist Giovanni Pierlugi, (1524-94) also known as Palestrina, wrote more than ninety Masses and scores of other musical pieces for religious occasions.

Of the many religious literary authors, Luigi Tansilio (1510-65) and Erasmo Valvasone were two of the most notable. Many of their religious themes were put to music and were popular with the Singing Guilds. The Singing Guilds were evening processions visiting the villages singing hymns of penitence and adoration. It is believed these Guilds did not perform outside of Italy.

The combination of these outside influences provided a colorful background of the times into which the church was developing.

CONSTANTINE, THE FIRST CHRISTIAN ROMAN EMPEROR (270-337)

The world has no scarcity of kings, emperors, generals, philosophers, etc. who have left their imprint on mankind. However none left a more impressive legacy than Emperor Constantine of the Roman Empire. His decisive act stands near the apex of those having the greatest and most widespread reaction. It now reaches out to one third of the world's population.

In 312 Constantine faced his arch-rival Maxentius, at the Milvian Bridge north of Rome, for a battle that would decide who would be emperor. Constantine was hesitant at first, but then he experienced a vision. He described it as seeing a cross in the sky with these words, "By this you shall conquer." He did not understand its meaning, but his soldiers marked their armor and shields with a "cross" and went into battle, winning a decisive victory against superior forces. (This is all the more remarkable because at that time the "cross" was not yet known as a symbol of Christianity.)

Constantine's family (including his mother St. Helena) was converted to Christianity and in 313 he proclaimed the "Edict of Milan" (also sometimes called The "Edict of Toleration") By this Edict Christianity became the official religion of the Roman Empire. (For details of the Edict, refer to section "Early Historical Influences.")

Constantine then took an active part in the affairs of the Church. (He was baptized prior to his death in 337) Despite a threatening schism, he wrote the following letter to the Bishops:

"Constantine, Emperor, to the Bishops of the Great Church:
My beloved brethren -- it must be clear to all men that nothing is more important to me than the fear of God. You have already planned to hold a synod of Ancyra in Galatia. Change your plans. Come to Nicea, a city in Bithynia. The Italian and European Bishops are coming already. Come to Nicea, it has excellent weather and I myself will be able to take part in and mark your discussions."

The following two quotations describe the depth and breadth of Christianity as of today, that so humbly began two thousand years ago.

"Christianity has become the most potent single force in the life of mankind." (7 p. 7) "Christianity is now deeply rooted in the lives and cultures of approximately one third of the peoples of the world." (3 p. 5)

Western world history begins with the genius of the ancient Greeks and the coming of our Lord Jesus. It is carried to this day by many Italians who paved the way for those who have followed.

HELENA, MOTHER OF CONSTANTINE

Helena was born in Britain to a British Tribal King. Her mother was said to be a Roman woman living in Britain at the time of the Roman occupation of Britain. (This would make her one-half Italian.) She married Constantius, an officer in the Roman army, and their eldest son was Constantine, destined to become Roman Emperor Constantine. (This would make him three-quarters Italian heritage.)

Helena traveled to Rome with Constantine, where they lived until his adult life under her guidance and influence. After he became emperor, he declared her Empress and bestowed other honors upon her.

She converted to Christianity and traveled to Jerusalem in search of the True Cross. (She could be referred to as the world's first archeologist.) Her search produced what was believed to be the True Cross and thorns and nails. The relics were returned to Rome and are displayed in the Church of St. Croce (often referred to as Church of St. Helena, Rome.) She was later canonized as St. Helena. Since by heritage Constantine is three-quarters Italian, and was raised and Italianized in Rome, Italy has claimed him one-hundred percent as their own.

Relics Retrieved from the Holy Land by Helena, Mother of Emperor Constantine, and Brought to Rome.

The Relics are on display in the Church of St. Croce in Rome. (Also known as the Church of St. Helena.)

The search by Helena was made approximately 275 years after the crucifixion of Christ. The burial site of the Cross was well known as it was the scene of frequent pilgrimages. The same was true of many other important burial grounds, such as those of the followers of Christ. As any visitor to the catacombs knows, many bodies were placed in a hollowed-out nitch in the walls and then bricked up. Removing the bricks revealed the remains. Many, in the meantime, had been canonized and often their remains were reburied in churches named in their honor throughout the world.

The time of her search was not inordinately long after the events. In a comparable time frame, it would represent a time period of approximately fifteen years prior to the birth of George Washington to the present time. The Relics retrieved by Helena, while subject to some question, could very well be authentic under the circumstances of their recovery.

EPILOGUE

Christianity, as we know, did not originate in Italy. In Book I we state similarly that civilization and culture also did not originate in Italy. However, Italy's contribution was the translation and perfection of these early concepts, and they became their legacy to future generations.

Every nation at one time or another has had a part in the spread of Christianity. None was as sustaining, century after century, as Italy's; and it was Italy that, time after time, provided innovation and imagination at critical periods, to advance the dreams and aspirations of mankind.

Italy was in the forefront of the spread of Christianity which has become the world's greatest influence on mankind. Christopher Dawson (Professor of Roman Catholic Studies at Harvard) states, "Christianity was propagated from Rome." It is worthy to note that of the many and vigorous forces challenging Christianity such as Marx, Engles, Darwin, Schopenhauer and Carlyle, to mention only a few, none of the anti-Christians were Italians.

"Italy, conceived and willed by God as the land in which His Church should be centered, has been the object of His special love and extraordinary Providence, because no other people has, as the Italian people, its destinies so closely united with the work of Christ." (John Navone, S.J., Gregoriana University, Rome. *Italian Journal* 1991 (3, 4 vol. 5) (14 p.38)

BIBLIOGRAPHY NOTE ON EUSEBIUS

As to No. 22 - Eusebius wrote the only <u>surviving</u> history of Christianity of its first 300 years. It was written approximately 310 A.D. and has survived until this day. Great importance is ascribed to this work because of the crucial nature of the first 300 years of Christianity. Eusebius nearly lost his life because he was a Christian, but because of his friendship with Emperor Constantine, his punishment was banishment along with Pope Marcellinus. (Pope Marcellinus was later martyred.)

(33 p. 16) Eusebius was also Pope, 309-310. Eusebius - *The History of the Church From Christ to Constantine* - Translated by G.A. Williamson. Published by Dorset Press, N.Y. - 1965. (It can be purchased in any book store).

BIBLIOGRAPHY AND REFERENCES BOOK II

1. *The Early Christians*, Michael Gough. F/A/ Praeger Co. N.Y. 1961

2. *Erdman's Handbook to the History of Christianity* organizing Editor, Tom Dowley, W.D. Erdman Co. Grand Rapids, Michigan 1977.

3. *The History of Christianity, Beginning to 1500*, Scott Latourette, Revised Edition, Vol. I. Harper & Row Publishers, San Francisco 1975.

4. *Augustine of Hippo*, Peter Brown University of California Press, Berkeley, CA 1967.

5. *The Gateway to the Middle Ages - Italy*, Eleanor S. Duckett, Dorsett Press. University of Michigan, 1938 and 1966.

6. *National Geographic "Tapestry of History and Map" and "History of Europe*, National Geographic Society Books Division, Washington, D.C.

7. *A History of Christianity Vol. II*. Reformation to the Present Revised Edition, Kenneth S. Latourette, Harper & Row Publishers, N.Y. 1975.

8. *A History of the Popes*, Nicholas Cheetam, Dorsett Press, N.Y. 1982.

9. *Lives of the Saints*, Rev. Hugo Hoever, S.O. Cist. Catholic Book Publishing Co., N.Y. 1976 (p. 28)

11. *The Mary Noll Daily Missal*, A.J. Kennedy & Sons Co., N.Y. 1964 Edition.

12. *The Christians and the Roman Empire*, Marta Sordi of Milan, Italy. Translated by Anabel Beldini, University of Oklahoma Press, Norman Oak, Ok. 1986.

13. *The Bad Popes*, E.R. Chamberlain. Dorsett Press, N.Y. 1909

14. *The Italian Journal* - The Italian Academy Foundation, Inc. 278 Clinton Ave. Dobbs Ferry, N.J. 10522, Victor Tesoro, Founder & Chairman. Annual subscription $36.00 [A "must" in every Italian household.]

15. *Encyclopedia Britannica* - Detailed Study Series, 1989, Editor.

16. *The Christian Centuries*, Gumley and Redhead. B.B.C. Books Ltd., - London, 1989.

17. *Memoirs of Emperor Handrain*, M. Yourcner Farrar, Straus Co., N.Y. 1963.

18. *Arab History of the Crusades*, Francesco Gabriel, Dorset Press, N.Y. 1989.

19. *The Making of the Christian World, From Christ to the Renaissance*, 1990.

20. *The Triumph of the West*, J.M. Roberts, B.B.C. Books, Ltd. London 1985

21. *The World's Great Religions*, Time Books, Inc., N.Y. 1957

22. *The History of the Church from Christ to Constantine*, by Eusebius, 300 A.D. Translated by C.A. Williamson, Dorset Press, N.Y. 1965.

23. *The Great Betrayal*, Ernie Bradford, Dorsett Press, N.Y. 1967.

24. *Great People of the Bible and How They Lived*, Reader's Digest Book Division, N.Y. 1974.

ILLUSTRATIONS

Photo Source (16.)

Constantine, son of Constantius, was a battle-wise soldier with a broken Roman nose and proud of his rugged handsomeness.

He was fond of and respected his mother, Helena. He declared her empress and struck a medal in her honor. He feared and searched for a strong God, was the first Roman Emperor to be baptized a Christian, and called a halt to the persecution of Christians throughout the Empire.

He credits his great victory at the Battle of the Milvian Bridge to a vision he experienced prior to the battle. He tells of seeing a "cross" in the sky with the inscription, "By this you shall conquer." He says he did not understand its meaning, but they marked their armor and shields with the sign and won a crucial battle against superior forces. By this victory he became the Emperor.

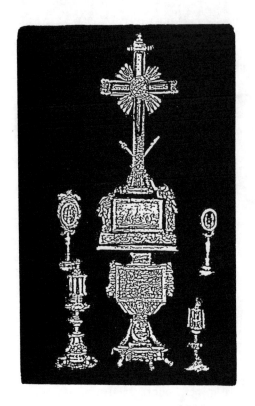

Relics Brought Back By Helena

The Relics brought back by Helena and illustrated here
are as follows:
1. A piece of the True Cross (visible behind the glass
   in the reliquary cross)
2. A portion of the Inscription (in partial decay)
   Bottom center.
3. A large nail removed from the Cross. (Lower left)
4. A bone fragment from the hand of St. Thomas.
   (Upper left)
5. Two thorns. (Upper right)
6. The object in the lower right portion of the display
   was not identified clearly. (Lower right)

Relic the True Cross

(Visible Inside the Cross behind the Glass)

A Portion of the Inscription

Nail Removed from the Cross
found in the burial site

Two Thorns Found in the Grave Site Where
The True Cross was believed to have been
buried.

Bone Fragments from the Hand of The Apostle St. Thomas

PRINCIPAL ROADS OF THE ROMAN EMPIRE

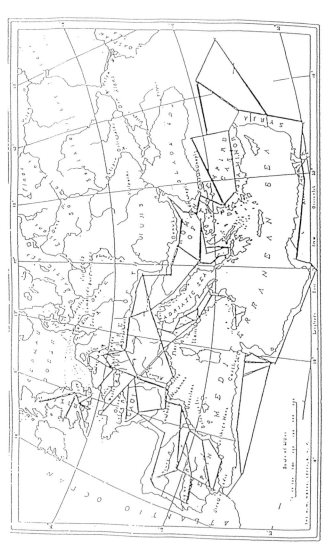

Roads of the Roman Empire consisted of approximately 50,000 miles of first class roads and approximately 200,000 miles of secondary roads

In 350 A.D. travel from Persia to Spain (3000 miles) took approximately 14 days, this was never equaled again anywhere in the world until the early 1900's.

INDEX OF
ITALIAN SAINTS
(Partial List)

INDEX OF MONASTERIES AND ORDERS FOUNDED
BY ITALIAN RELIGIOUS VOCATIONS

S.

V.

INDEX
ITALIAN POPES

INDEX